Sparks from Fireflies

A night light for the darkest nights.

By: the Ladies of Girl Scout Troop #1980

Sparks from Fireflies

kindness · Peace · Love · Hope

By: The Ladies of Girl Scout Troop #1980

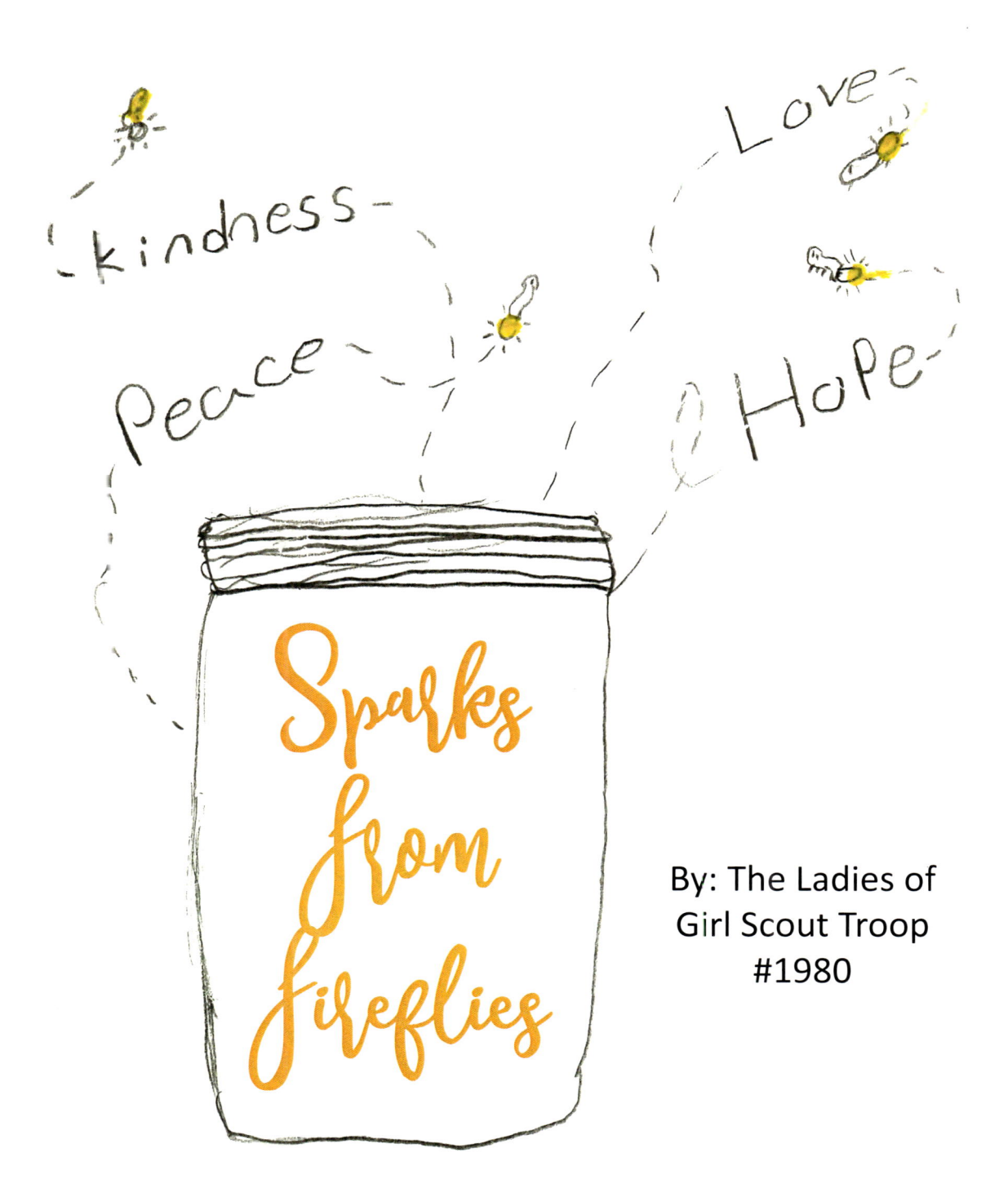

A night light for the darkest nights.

BOOKLOGIX®

Alpharetta, GA

All rights reserved. No part of this book may be reproduced or transmitted in any form or by any means, electronic or mechanical, including photocopying, recording, or any information storage and retrieval system, without permission in writing from the author.

Copyright © 2020 by Lisa McAbee

ISBN: 978-1-63183-705-0

10 9 8 7 6 5 4 3 2   0 2 1 1 2 0

Printed in the United States of America

∞This paper meets the requirements of ANSI/NISO Z39.48-1992 (Permanence of Paper)

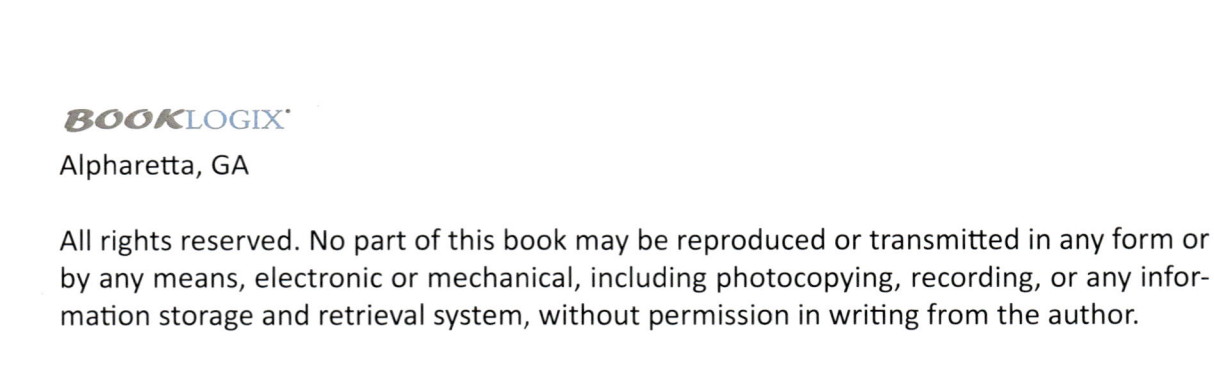

Artwork Credit: The Authors artistic creations used with permission
Cover Art: Marin McAbee, used with permission

Dedication

Sparks from Fireflies was designed to help children find their light in the dark.

Dedicated to **Mrs. Penny E. Warren.**

Thank you for all the love, support, and guidance to the authors. She knew what we could achieve before we even began.

Penny E. Warren
4/17/20

This page was intentionally left blank by the publisher.
Draw your name, or a self portrait here, on this page.

"A bend in the road is not the end of the road, unless you fail to make the turn."
~ Helen Keller

This page was intentionally left blank by the publisher.
Draw your own firefly, or several, right here on this page.

Preface

Working with Girl Scouts and the ladies of Girl Scout Troop #1980 is more about reminding myself to stay positive and seek joy in even the very difficult moments. Working with Girl Scouts reminds me of how important each of us are and how much stronger we become as a group.

The pages of this book had been in my hands for almost a year before they came together in a book. Each girl brought forward quotes they personally use as motivation and some added illustrations to emphasize the message. It has been a joy to watch this book come together, to guide the process and shape their ideas into what is now known as *Sparks from Fireflies*.

I wish you all joy along your adventure and hope this collection becomes a foundation you return to again and again. You are all powerful.

—Troop Leader Lisa

This page was intentionally left blank by the publisher.
Write your middle name as big as you can on this page. Color it in!

Introduction

The authors of this book, Girl Scout Troop #1980, were working on their Girl Scout Silver Award in 2019. As a group, they decided to serve a local non-profit agency, SafePath Children's Advocacy Center of Cobb County, Georgia (www.safepath.org).

The Troop decided they wanted to serve children in their community by helping to make their days as regular as any of their peers. Quickly, the Troop designed and assembled motivational quotes and drawings as Sparks for the reader.

And that is how *Sparks from Fireflies* began.
Let this collection be "a night light for the darkest nights" and your brightest days.

The Troop goal is to provide a book for every child served by SafePath in Cobb County Georgia, until the need for the nightlight no longer exists.

This book has been designed by kids, for kids.
We dare you; customize it, color it, write in it, and share from it.
These are now your Sparks from Troop #1980's Fireflies.

Share, Draw, Create!

This page was intentionally left blank by the publisher.
What do you see when you look up at the right sky? Stars, Planets, Animals, or other shapes? Draw your night sky here!

So what are *Sparks*?

The ladies of Girl Scout Troop #1980 wanted to make a collection of quotes they like that make them happy when times are tough. They want to make you smile. So each quote, drawing, or coloring page they give you — we call each of those a Spark.

May it Spark something within you to share, smile, and be happy!

Why *fireflies*?

As a Troop, we like to camp outside in tents.
Have you ever done that?
There are a lot of sounds, scents, and living things to interact with.
We like Fireflies, because they light up the sky right where they are.
Fireflies make their own light, their own happy!
We want to be your Firefly.

What does this all mean to you as the reader?

We hope that you will like this collection of Sparks, add in your own style by coloring, drawing, writing, and sharing these Sparks with others. Making someone smile will make you happy, try it! We have made suggestions along the way of things to write, draw, or think about.

We invite you to read, interact, and enjoy this collection.
Go ahead and turn the page, we dare you!

take a moment to make a note of how you feel before we begin. Expressing your feelings in drawings and words is helpful

_____

_____

_____

_____

_____

_____

_____

_____

_____

what one word do you write most often?

Silver is precious,
Gold is too,
I am precious,
and so are YOU

draw something precious to you

write your name upside down and sideways, now doodle around it

You are ENOUGH just as you are

-Meghan Markle

BELIEVE IN YOURSELF

The true beauty lies within
-unknown

what is your favorite insect?
create your own bug here!

where do you like to day-dream? draw what you see when you day-dream

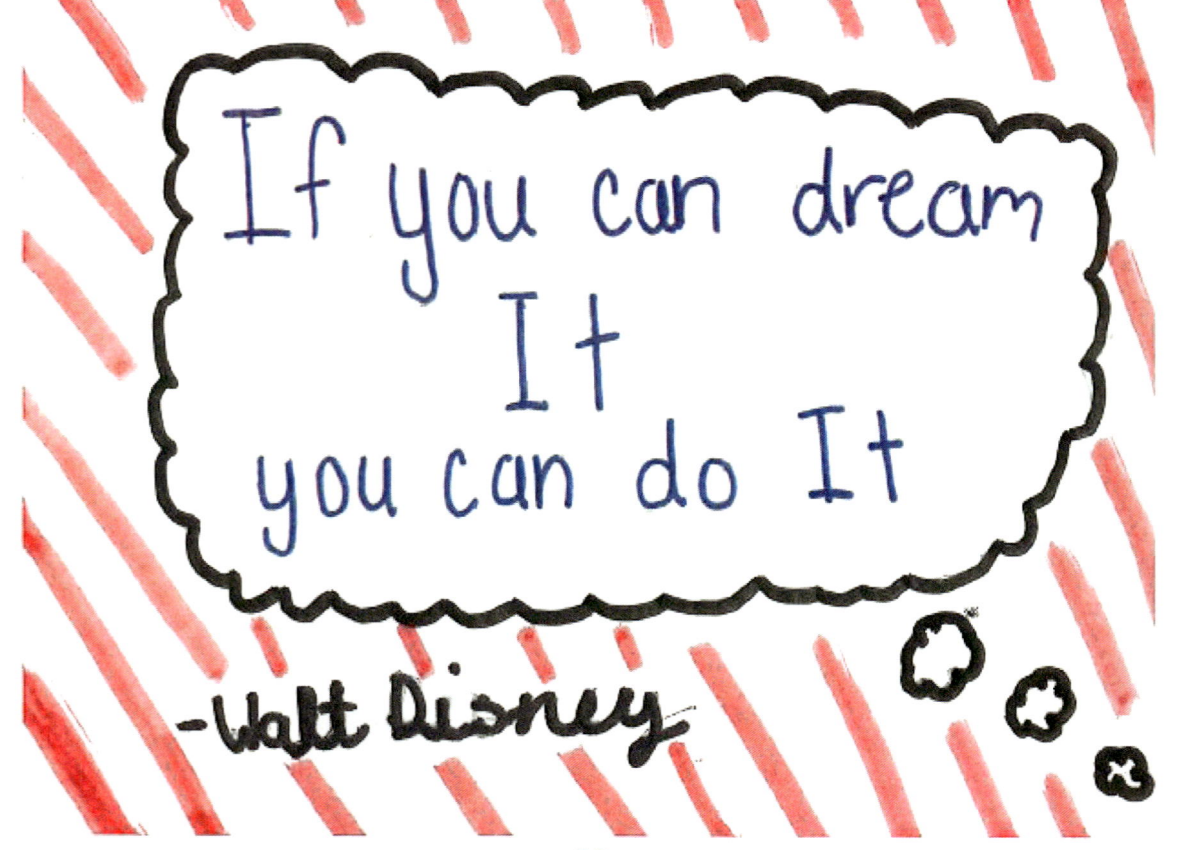

If you can dream It you can do It

—Walt Disney

You have a fingerprint no one else has.
So you can leave a mark no one else can.

Using a marker or ink pad, mark this page with your finger print.

Be the type of person who can smile on the worst day.

—Unknown

Look at your smile in a mirror, write about your smile...

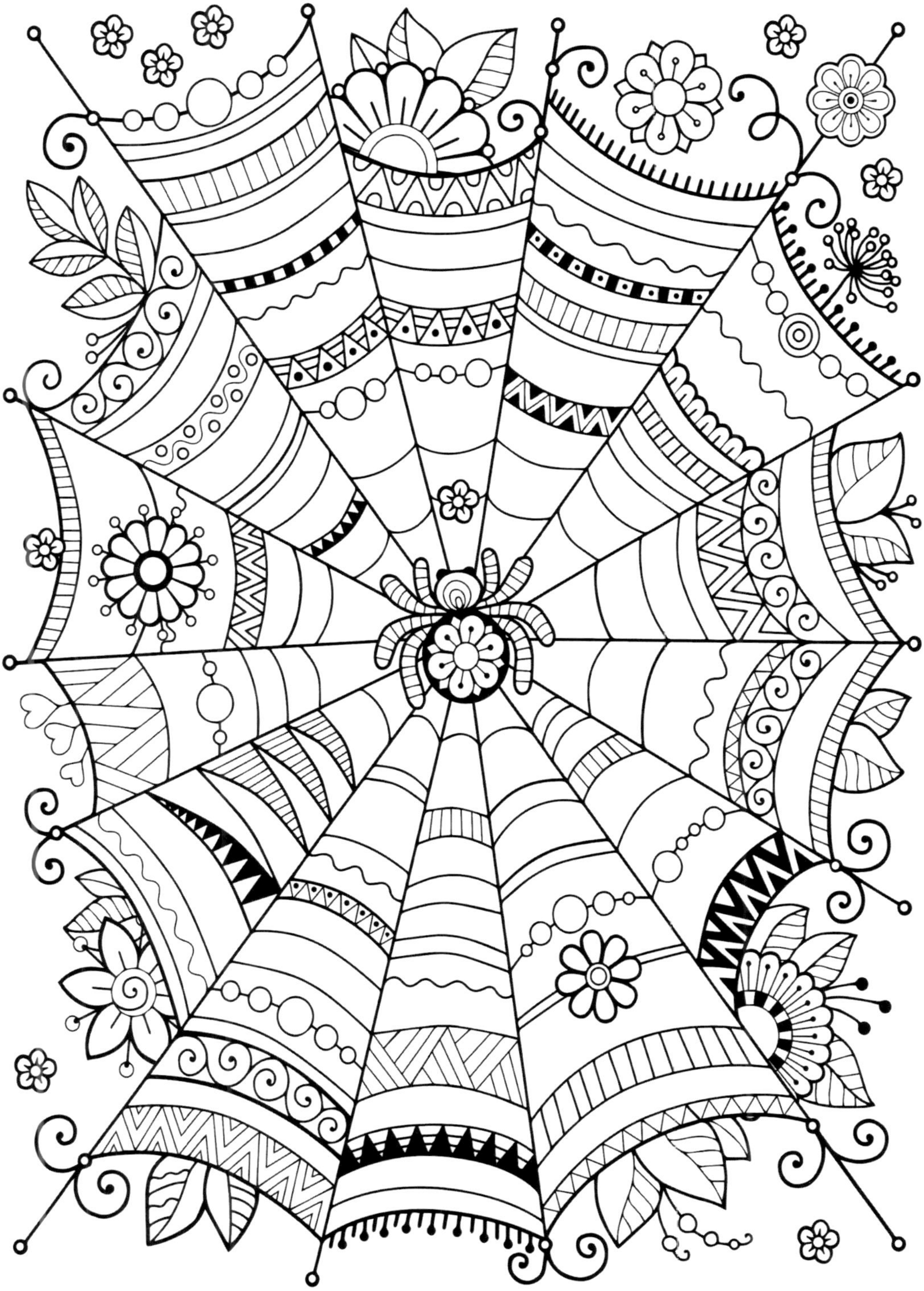

24

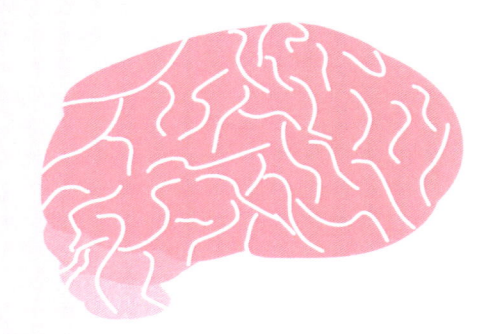

*Learn from yesterday,
Live for today,
Hope for tomorrow.*

- Albert Einstein

Albert Einstein was known for his big ideas. What are you known for?

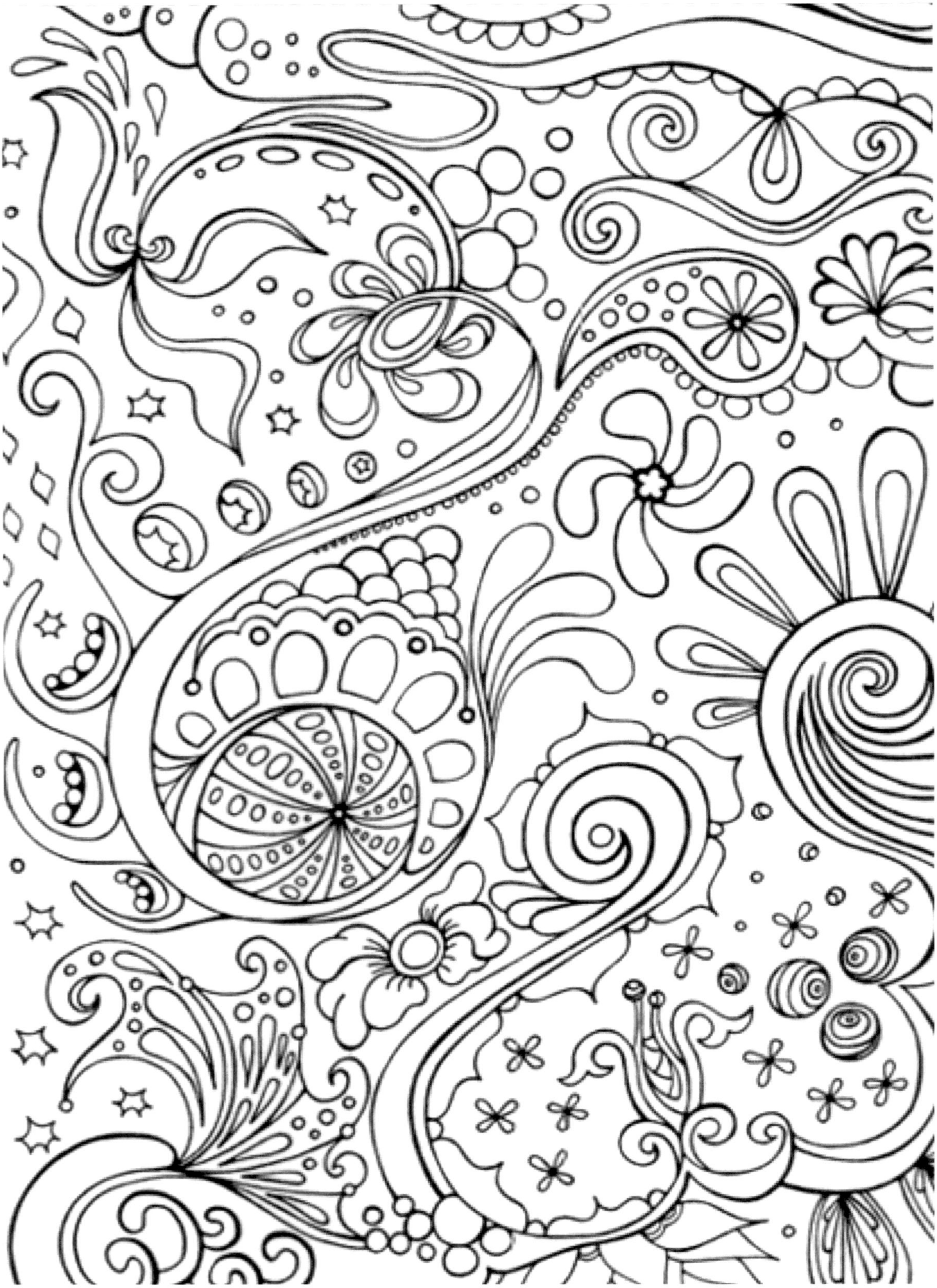

IF YOU'RE not *Smiling* you're doing it Wrong — Alex Wassbi

Smile at yourself in the mirror. Draw what your smile looks like here.

"Keep smiling, because life is a beautiful thing and there's so much to smile about."
—Marilyn Monroe

Who do you know that has the best smile? Write their name and draw their smile here.

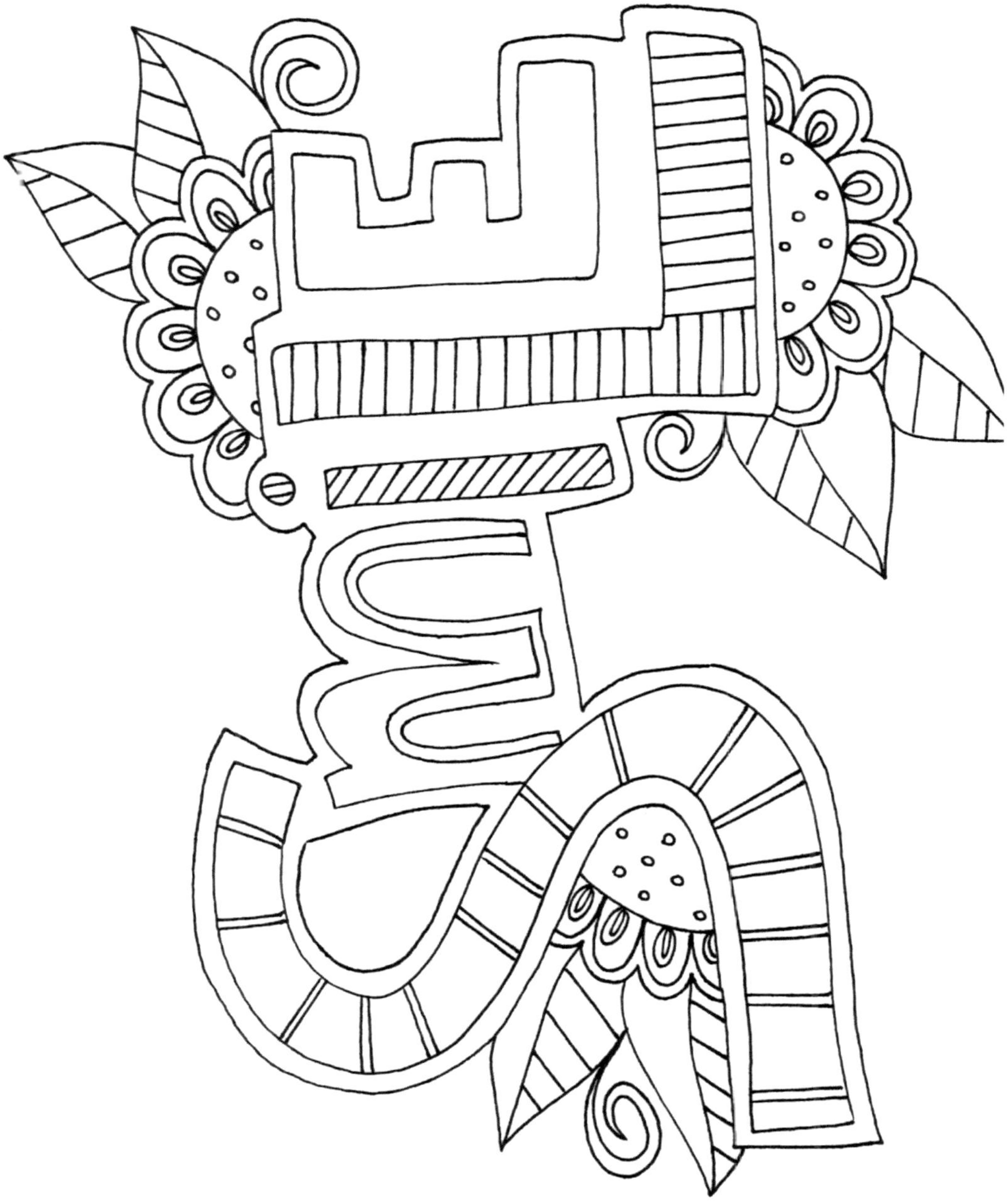

Can you make this drawing bigger? add to it with your drawings on this page.

add in words that make you happy.

> Only I can change my life. No one can do it for me.
> ~ Carol Burnett

tell someone a funny joke and watch their smile grow. did it make you smile? write the joke here to remember how funny you are.

Give each insect a funny name and share them with a friend.

Even The Toughest DOGS are afraid of vacuums.

i knew a dog named 'Stopit', have you heard a funny dog name? or can you make a funny name up!

> You MUST do the things you think you can not do.
> — Eleanor Roosevelt

what did you think you could not do but tried it anyway? write about it!

When the moon is out, look for footprints. Could the next footprint up there be yours?

Don't tell me the sky is the limit when there are footprints on the moon.

— Paul Brandt

Those who try to do something and fail, are infinitely better than those who try to do nothing and succeed.
— Lloyd Jones

Love Grows

SOME SEE WEEDS

I SEE WISHES

what was the last wish you made? who around you can make it come true?

if your wish came true would it make you happy?

if not, make another wish...

...and another wish

then, make one more wish...

You can't go back and change the beginning, but you can start where you are and change the ending.

—C.S. Lewis

think about how you want to change your story. make your story a comic book or a fantasy? write about it here!

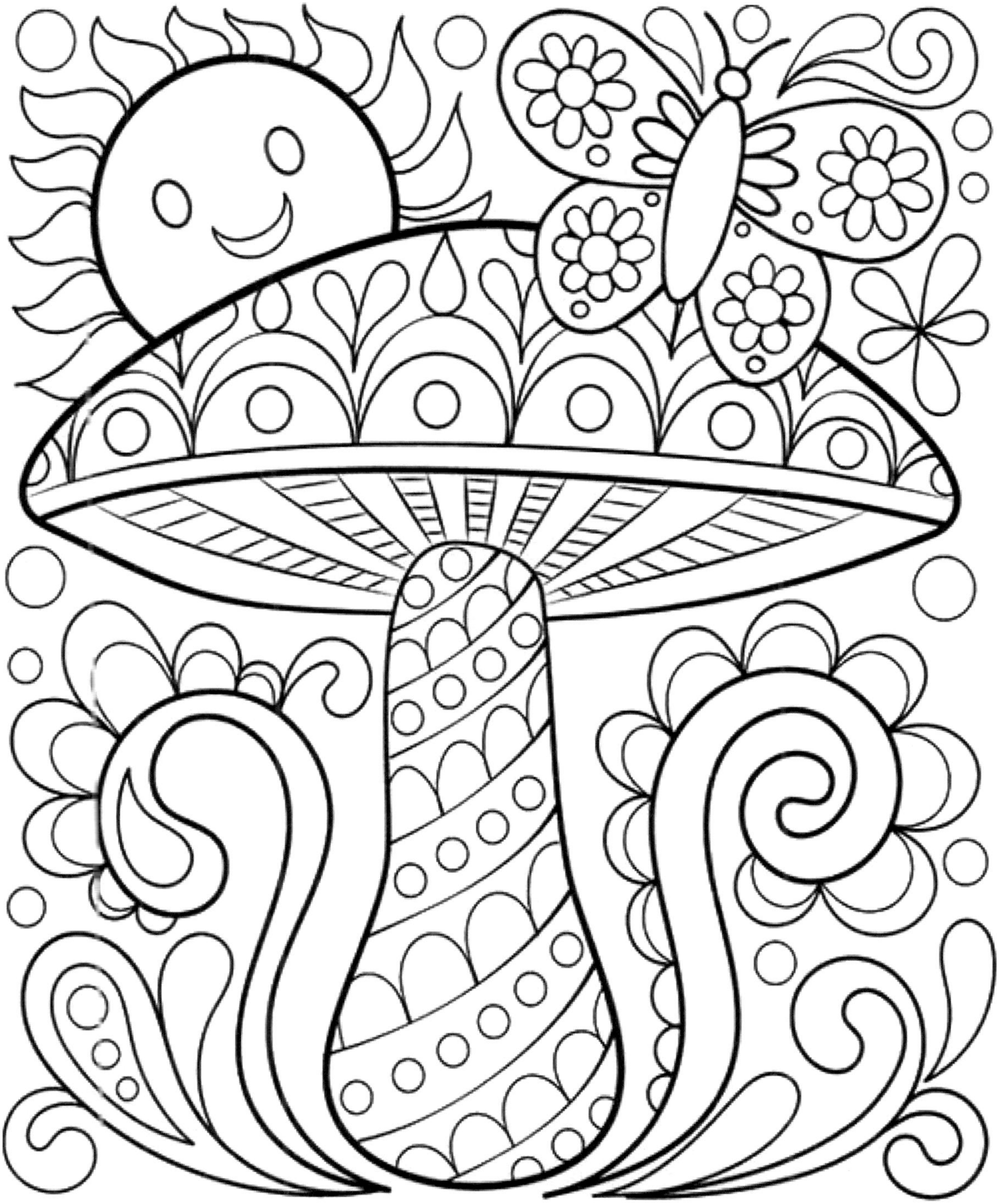

The journey of 1,000 miles begins with one step

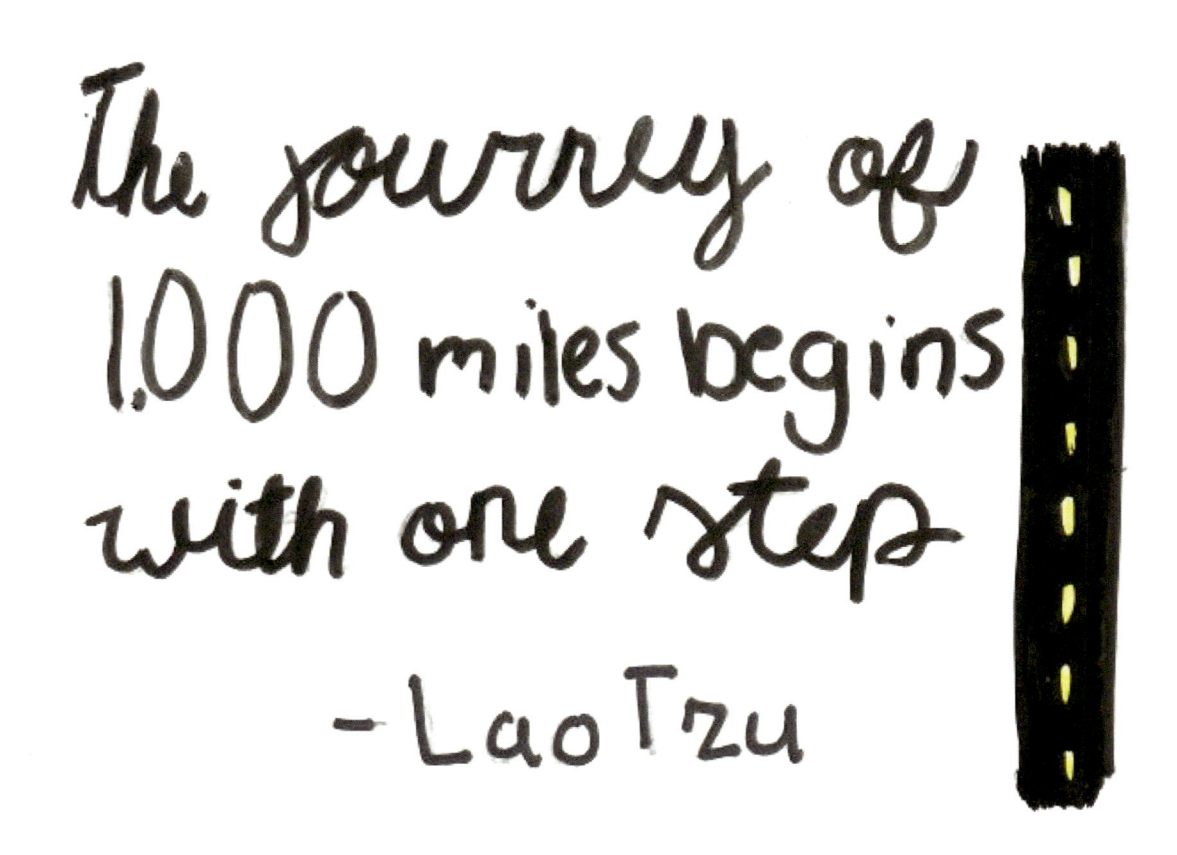

— Lao Tzu

what is 1,000 miles from you right now? check a map!

However difficult life may seem,

There is always something you can do and succeed at.
~ Stephen Hawking

I hope you don't mind,
that I put into words,
how wonderful life
is when you're in the
world.

— Bernie Taupin

Can you make your fingerprints into a few animals? give it a try...

fishies

> Do what is right not what is easy
> —anonymous

Write your name backwards, that is not easy to do!

I attribute my success to this: I never gave or took any excuse.

— Florence Nightingale

have you ever seen an owl outside, not in a zoo or in a cage?

are you perhaps a night owl too?

She was born to be free,
let her run wild in her own way
and you will never lose her.

~ Nikki Rowe

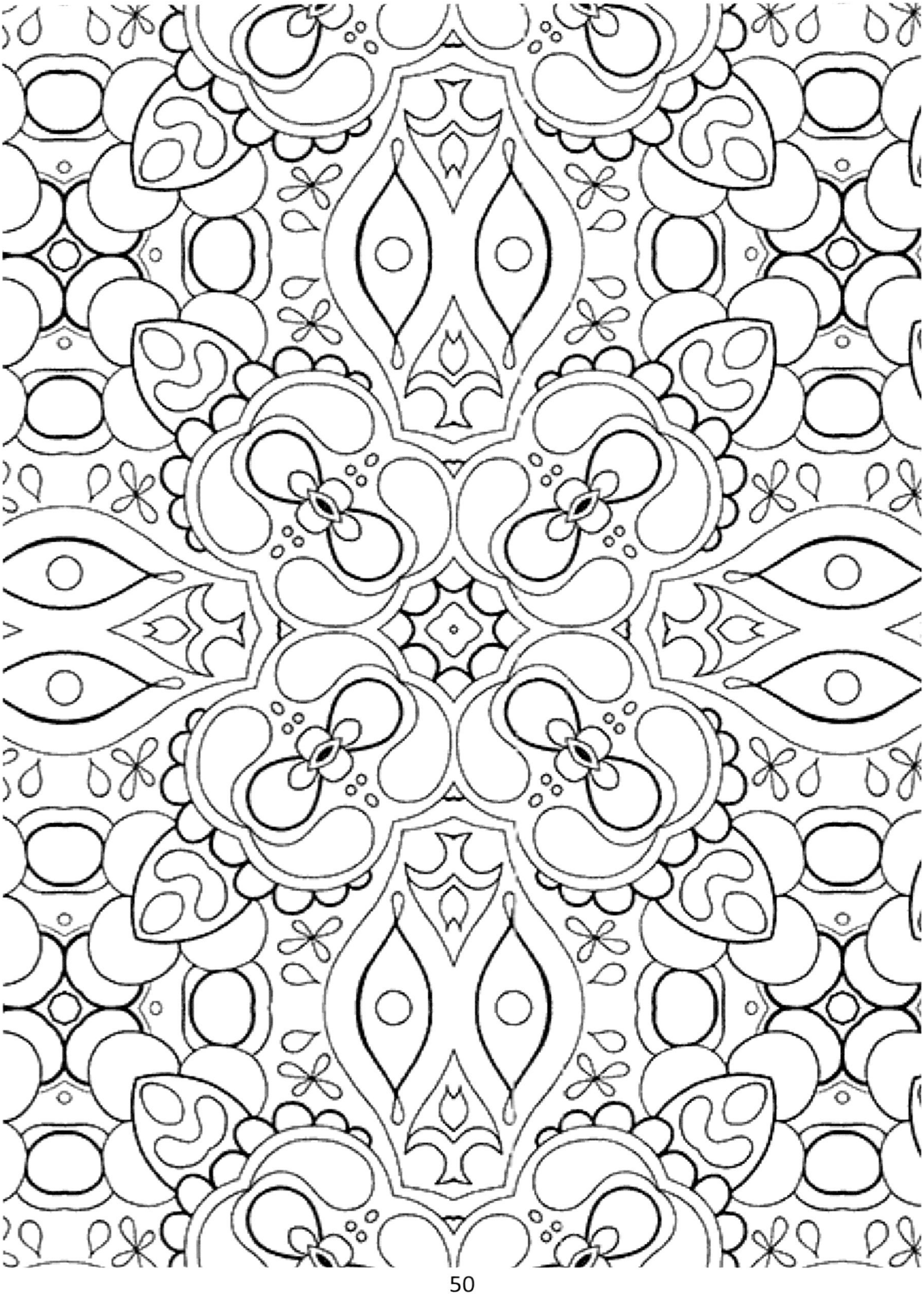

There's something about a woman with a loud mind that sits in silence, smiling knowing she can crush you with the truth

—R.G Moon

what is the longest you have held your breath? how about underwater?

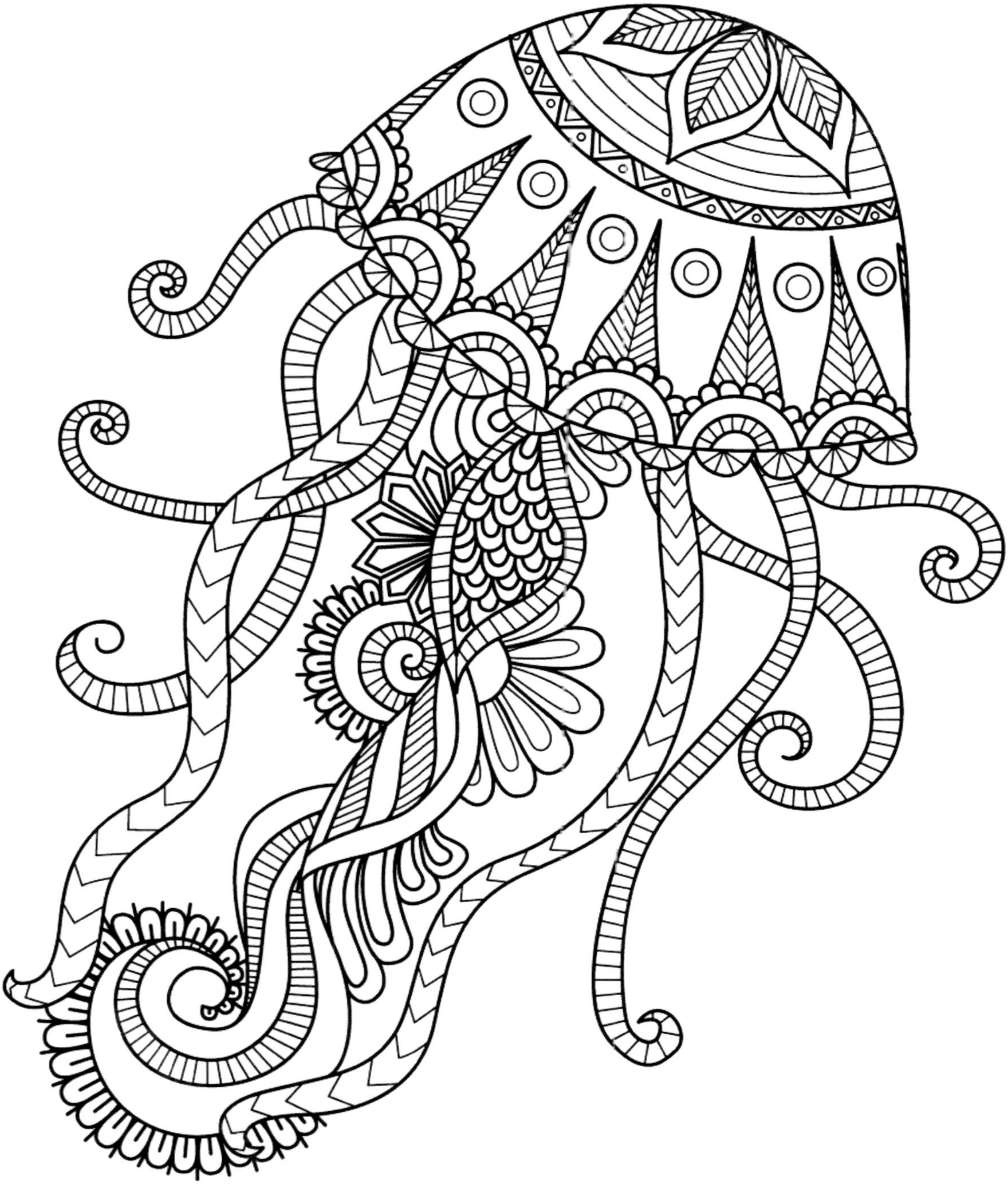

"Nothing is impossible the word it's self says I'm possible!"

—Audrey Hepburn

What did you think was impossible that you now know is easy?

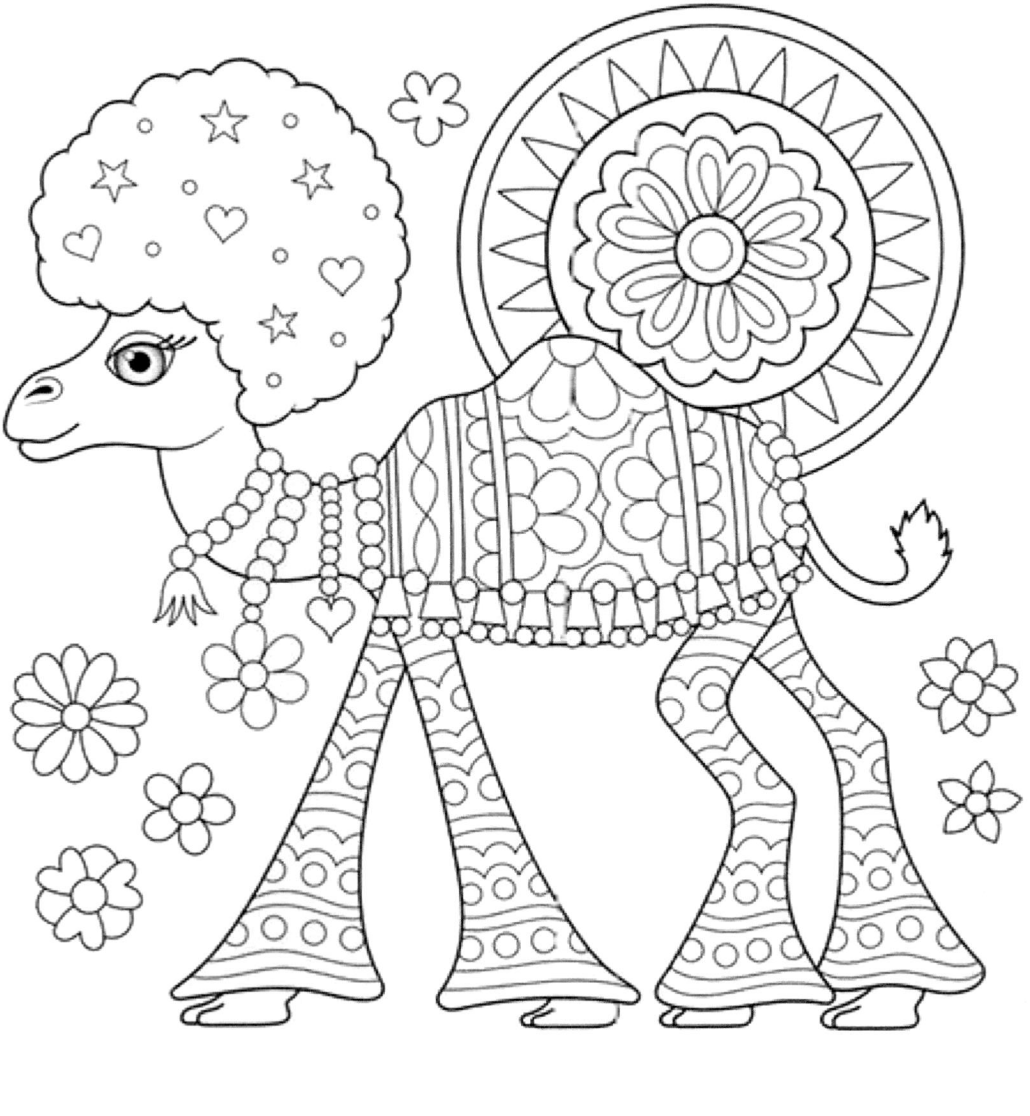

close your eyes.
think of your favorite food.
Open your eyes and write about why
you like that food.

_____

_____

_____

_____

_____

_____

_____

_____

_____

_____

who makes your favorite food?

"I've learned that no matter what happens, or how bad it seems today, life does go on, and it will be better tomorrow."

— Maya Angelou

What makes you different?
Your differences make you unique and strong. Write about it.

YOU HAVE BRAINS IN YOUR HEAD.

YOU HAVE FEET IN YOUR SHOES.

YOU CAN STEER YOURSELF

ANY DIRECTION YOU CHOOSE.

-DR. SEUSS

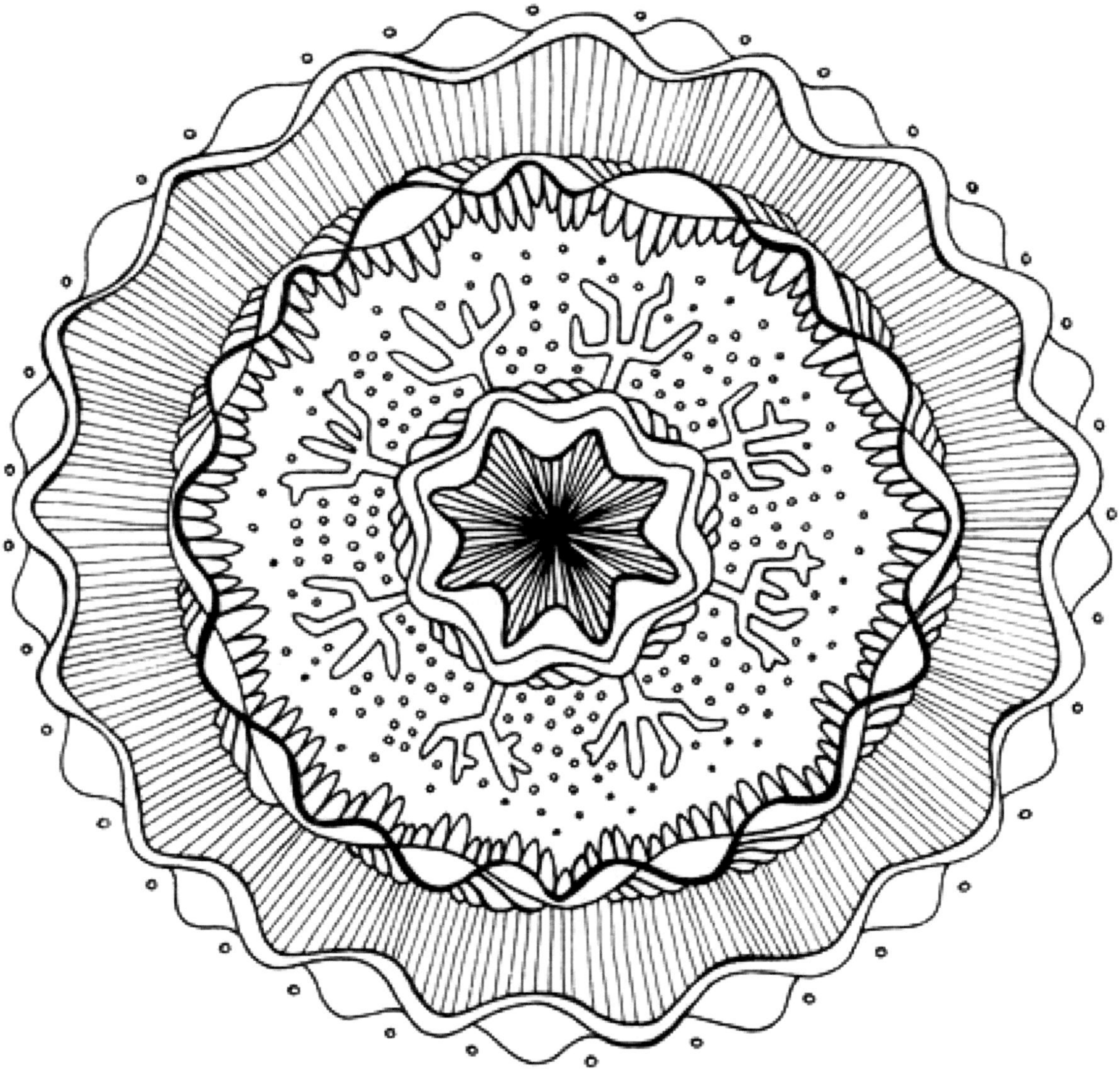

When you reach the end of your rope, Tie a knot in it and hang on!

— Proverb from the American West

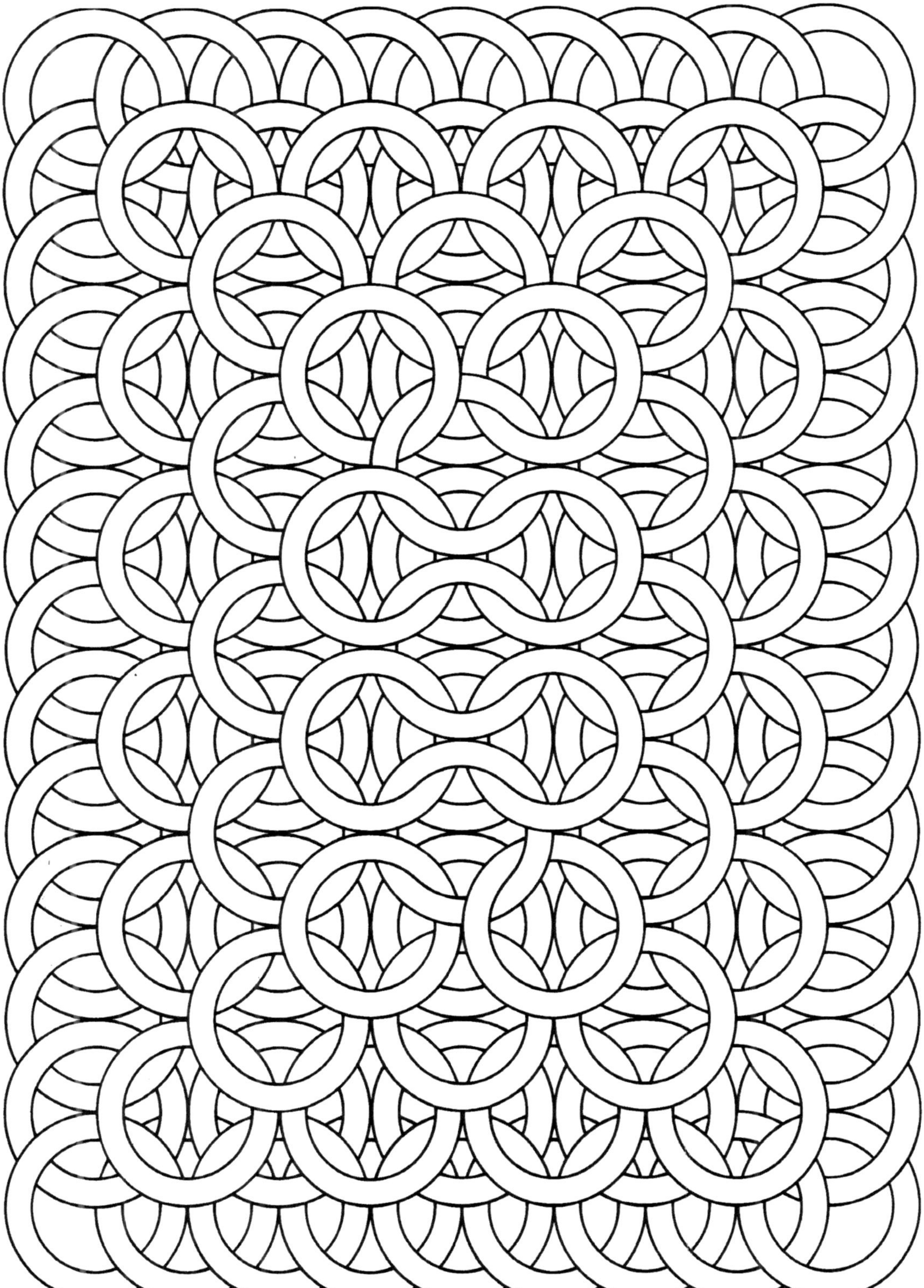

> It does not matter how slow you go as long as you don't give up
> — Confucius

have you ever tried to run faster than someone else? write about how you felt and if you won or not.

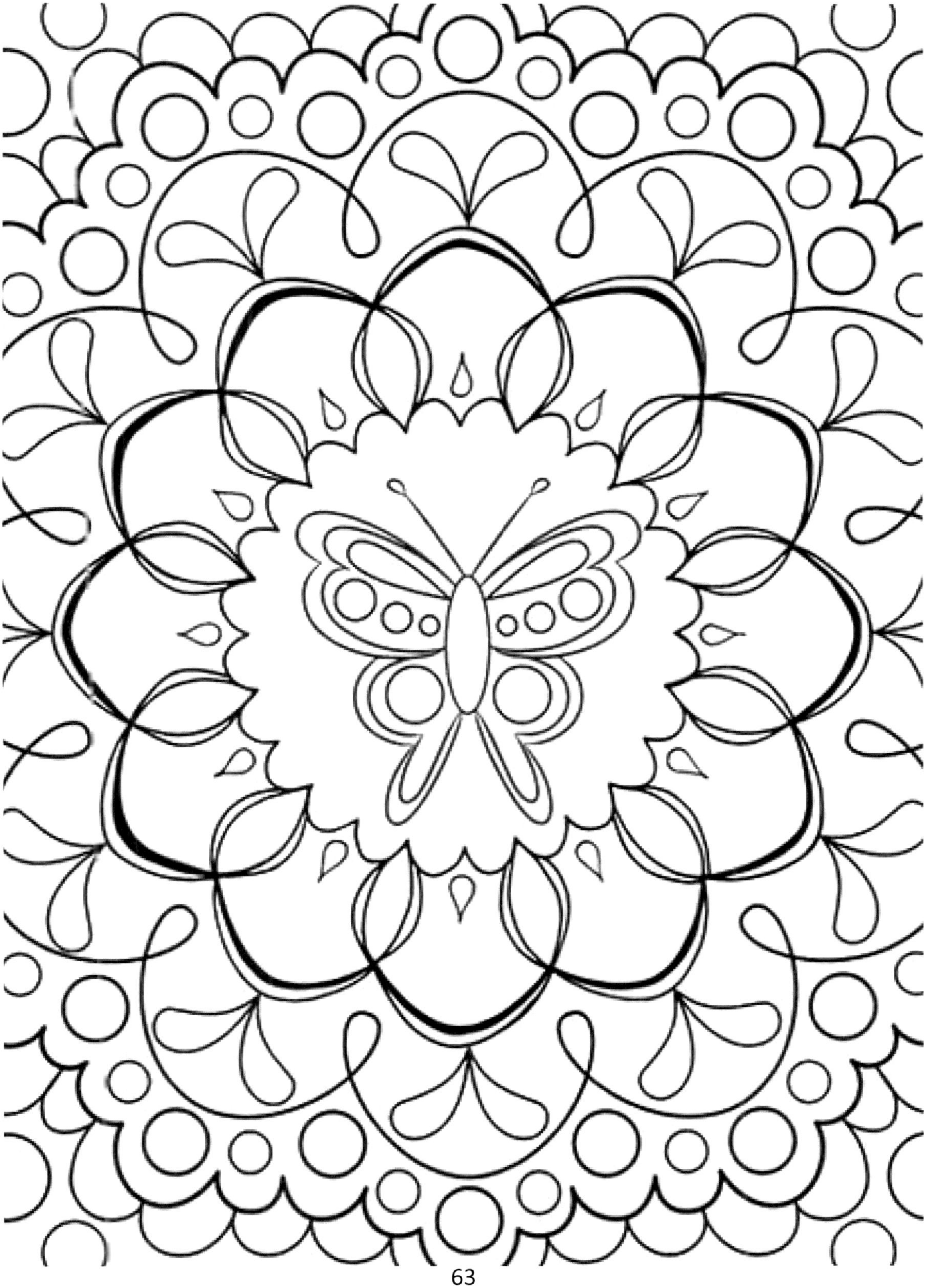

Don't let anything dull your Sparkle

—Doreen Virtue

How do you sparkle? Make a list of things that show your sparkle is different than anyone else.

Your day will go the way the corners of your mouth turn

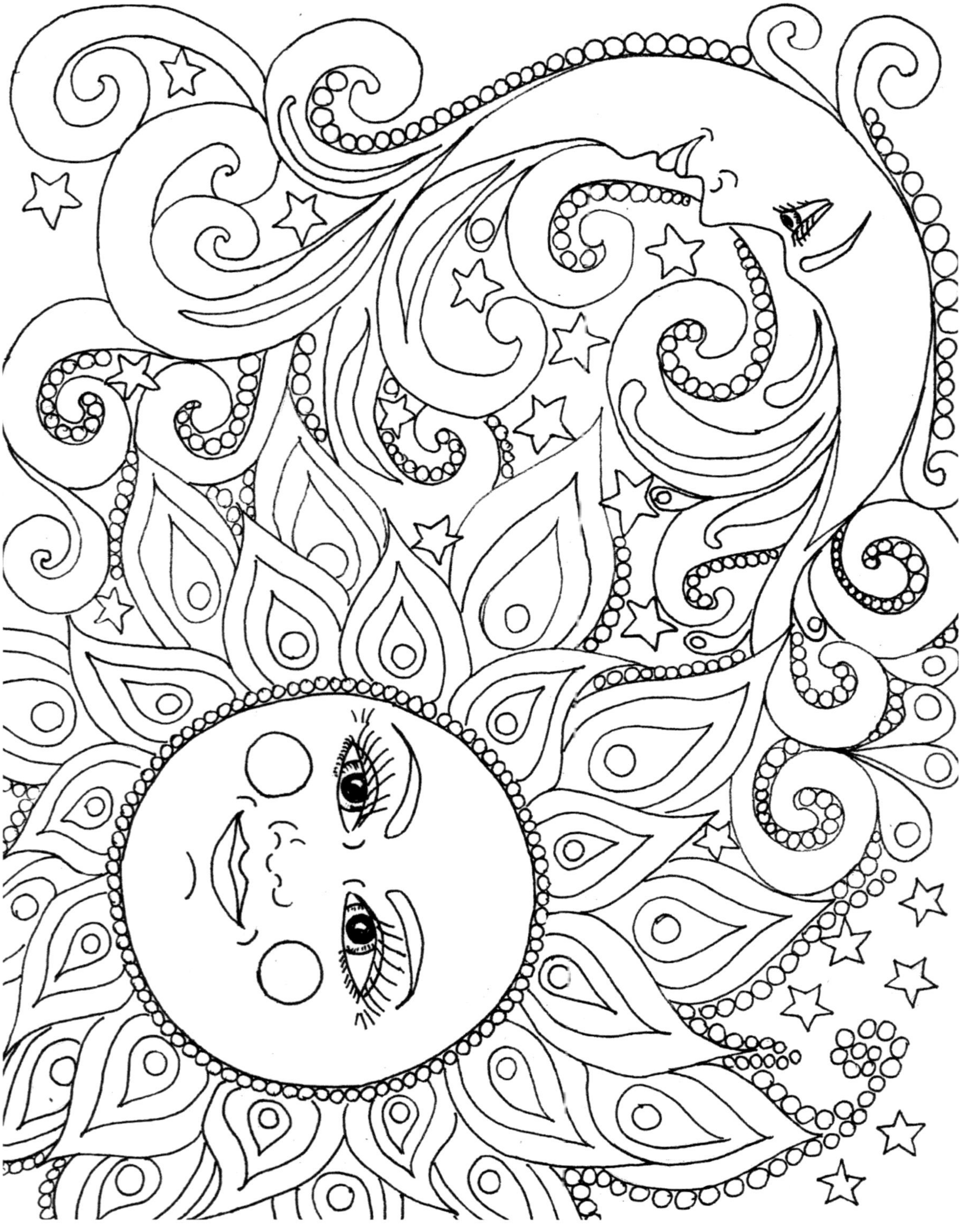

What sunshine is to flowers, smiles are to humanity.

—Joeseph Addison

Can you make another person laugh? be careful – smiles are contagious!

We Rise By lifting Others

—Hunting Louise

did you smile at someone else yet? try it today, it will lift someone else up!

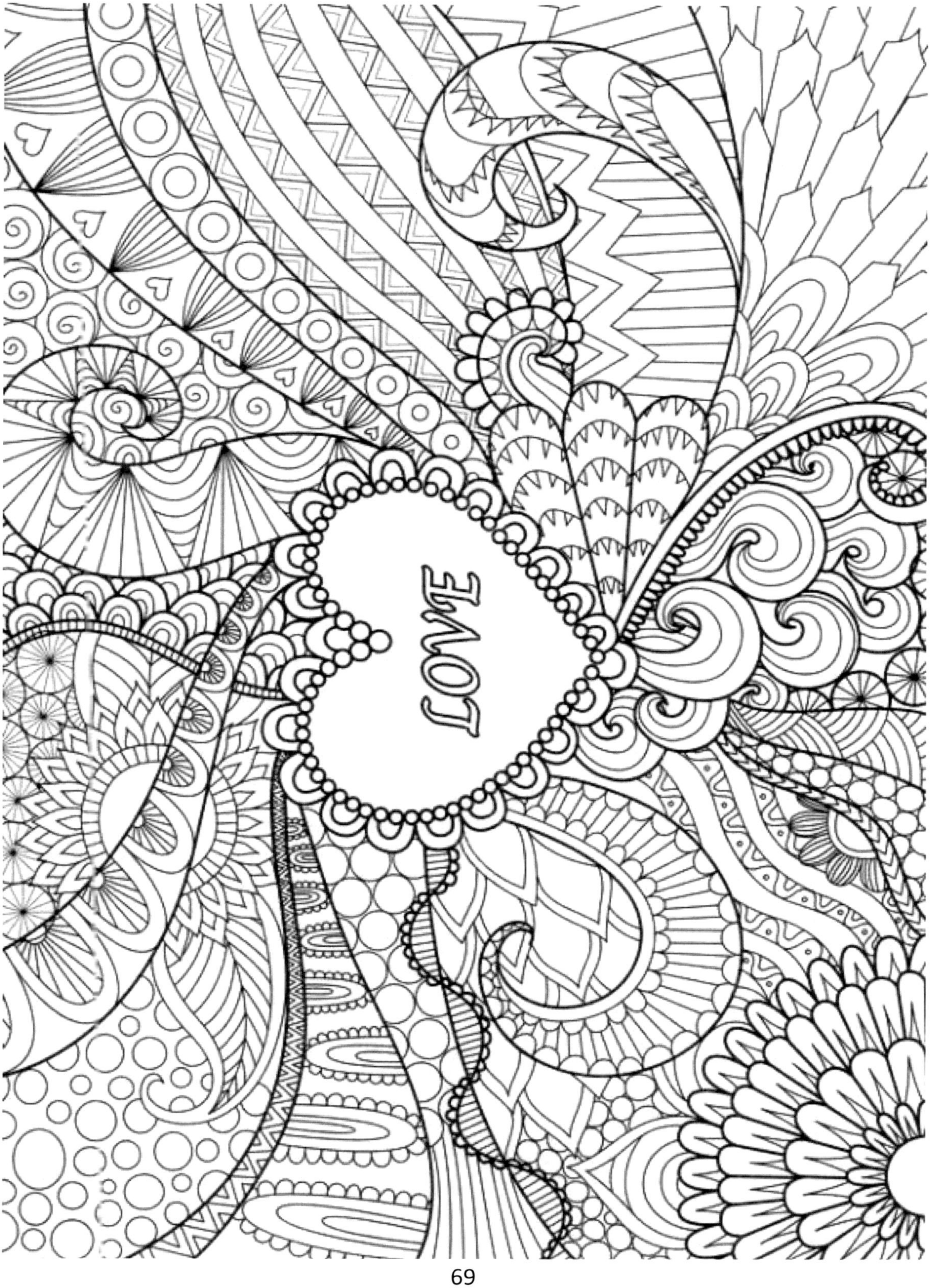
LOVE

Be the change you want to see in the world. —Gandhi

Positive thoughts about the roses, makes the thorns ok. Write a riddle about a positive way to see something...

You can complain because Rose bushes have thorns, or you can be grateful Thorn bushes have Roses

— J. Kenfield Morley

Outline a shadow on this page of something that you play with...

write about your shadow or your drawing.

> Keep your face towards the sunshine- and shadows will fall behind you
>
> —Walt Whitman

Where is your shadow right now? Is it taller than you or shorter?

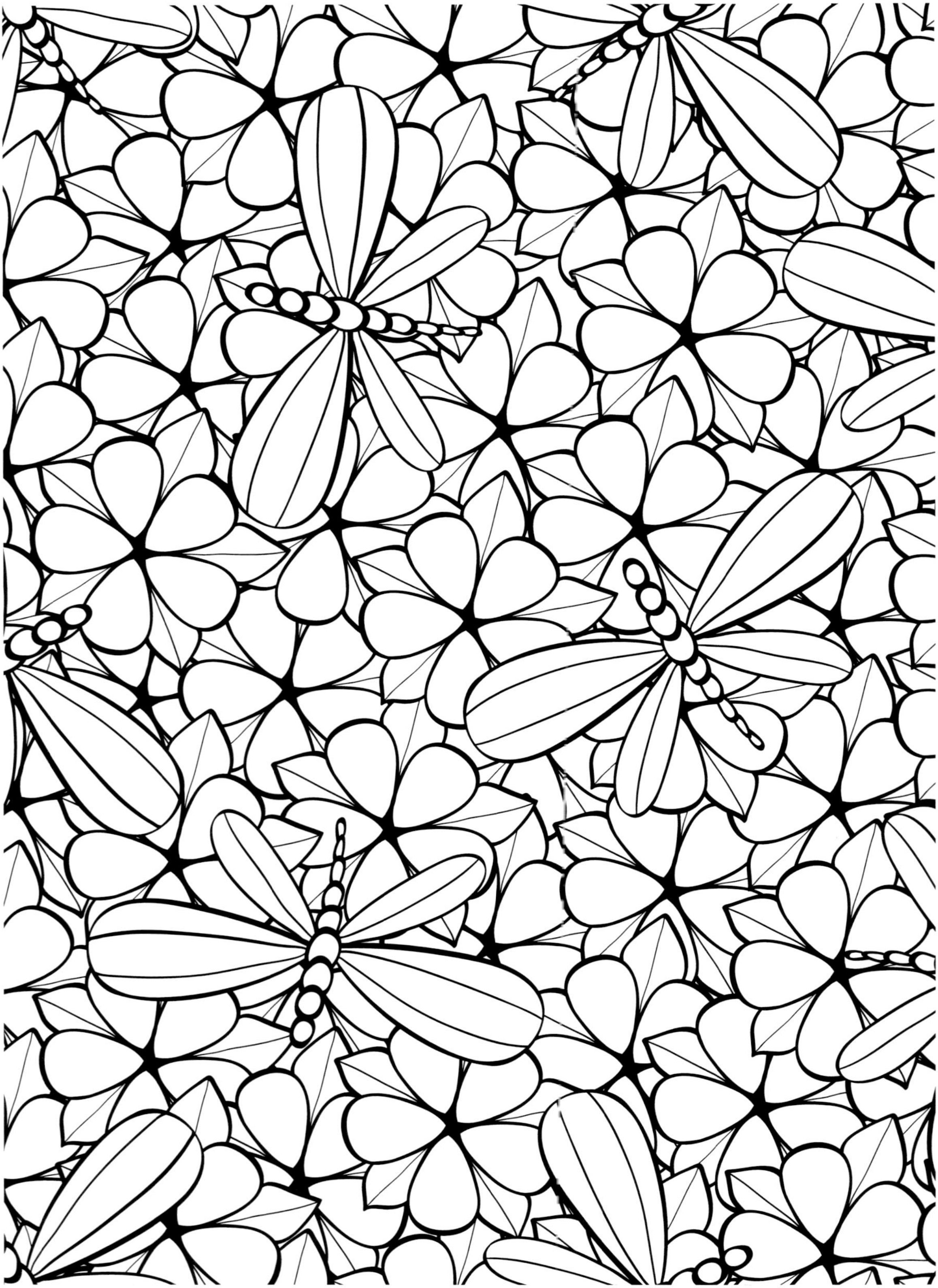

Aim for the moon. If you miss, you may still hit a star.

— W. Clement Stone

have you ever tried to count the stars in the night sky? give it a try...

Try to be a rainbow in someone else's cloud

Maya Angelou

have you ever watched tv in black and white only? it's really weird!
Color these pages with every color!

Life is about using the WHOLE BOX of crayons
~ RuPaul

how old do you think dragonflies live to be? how old will you live to be?

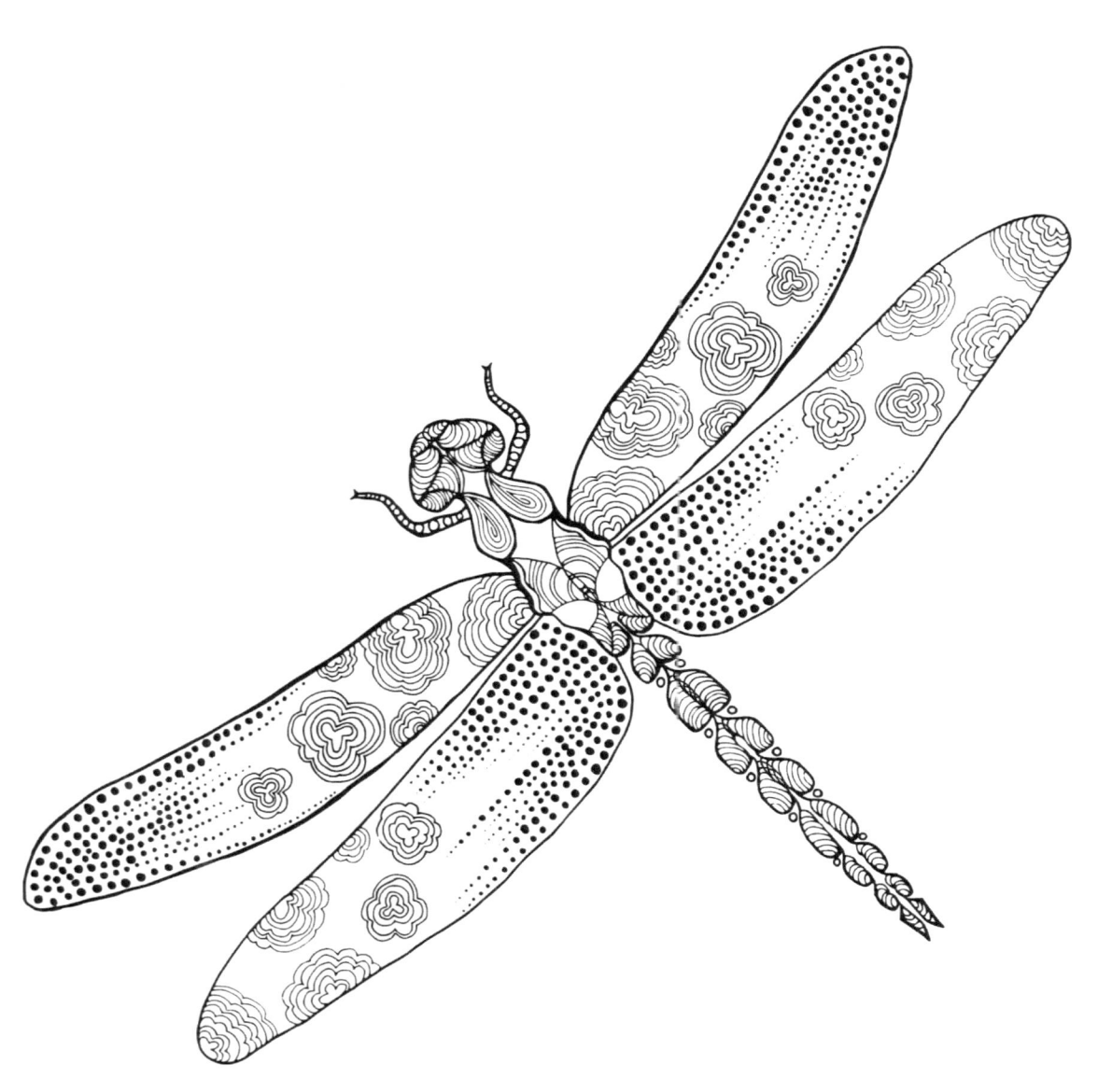

Never, Never, NEVER Give up!
—Winston Churchill

Next time on the monkey bars, try not to let go...

Don't wait. The time will never be just right.
-Napoleon Hill

Sometimes it's really hard to wait and sometimes it's not. what did you wait for that turned out amazing?

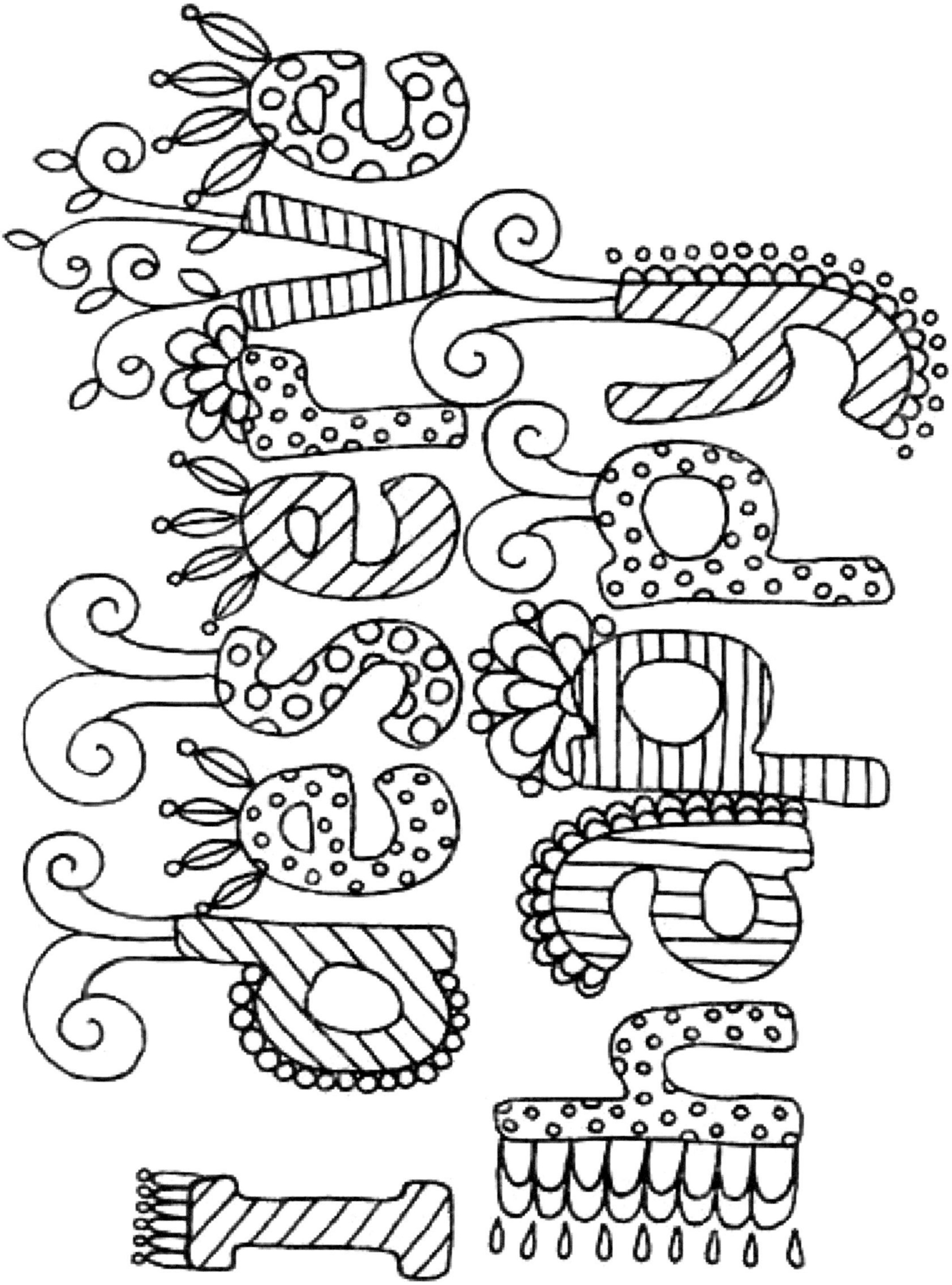
I deserve happy

There is only one thing that makes a dream impossible to achieve — the fear of failure.

~ Paulo Coelho

draw yourself doing your very best, what face do you make? do you stick out your tongue?

"Why worry? If you've done the very best you can, worrying won't make it any better."
— Walt Disney

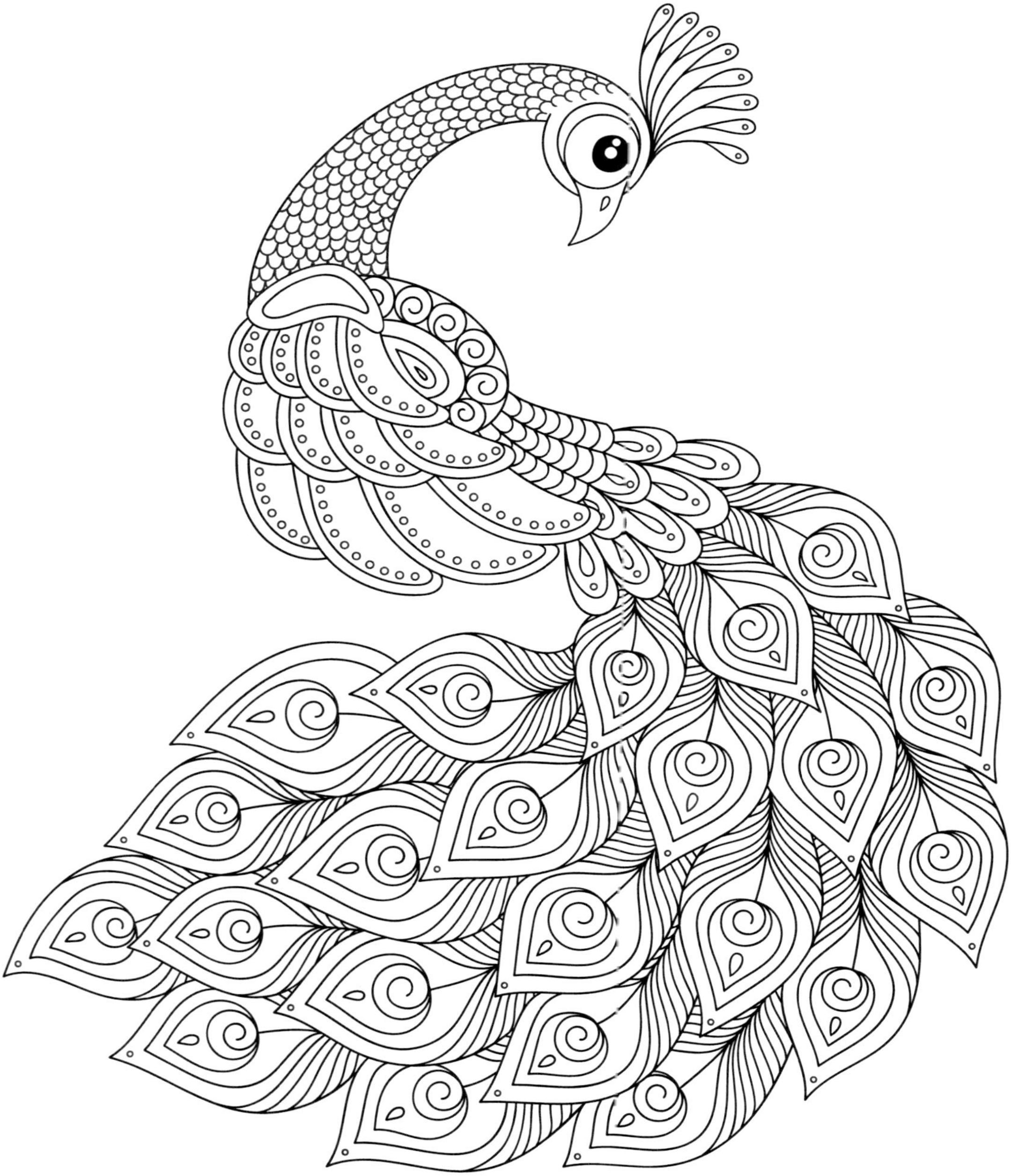

I learned that courage is not the absence of fear, but the triumph over it.

— Nelson Mandela

do you like bright sunny days? maybe rainy ones or the days in between?

Keep your face to the **SUNSHINE** and you cannot see a **SHADOW.** — Helen Keller

Each day is a gift, that is why they call it the present...

draw the greatest gift you ever gave someone else. Now, draw the greatest gift you ever received.

anne frank was a very brave girl and wrote about the troubles she faced in her lifetime. She belived in the power of positive writings...

take this space and the next page to write a powerful positive statement of your own.

"Whoever is HAPPY will make others HAPPY too."

— Anne Frank

that was powerful! share it with someone else to make them feel strong.

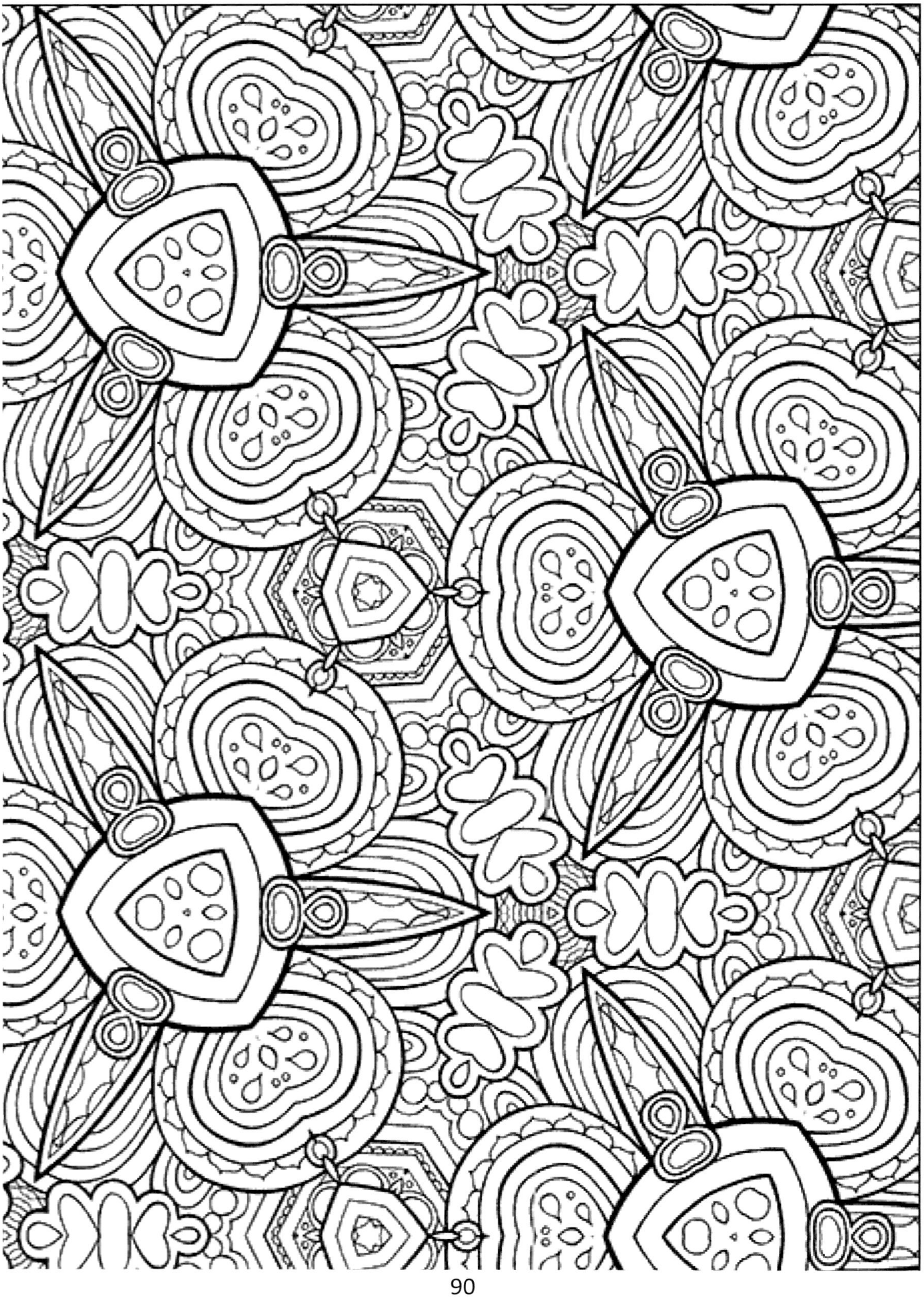

There is happiness in everything. You just have to **find it.**

what luck! - happiness is everywhere, what do you see right now that makes you happy?

Happiness and Confidence are the prettiest things you can wear.

—Taylor Swift

the HARDER the CONFLICT, the more GLORIOUS the TRIUMPH.

—Thomas Paine

School can be like this - hard work is always worth it. what do you like about school?

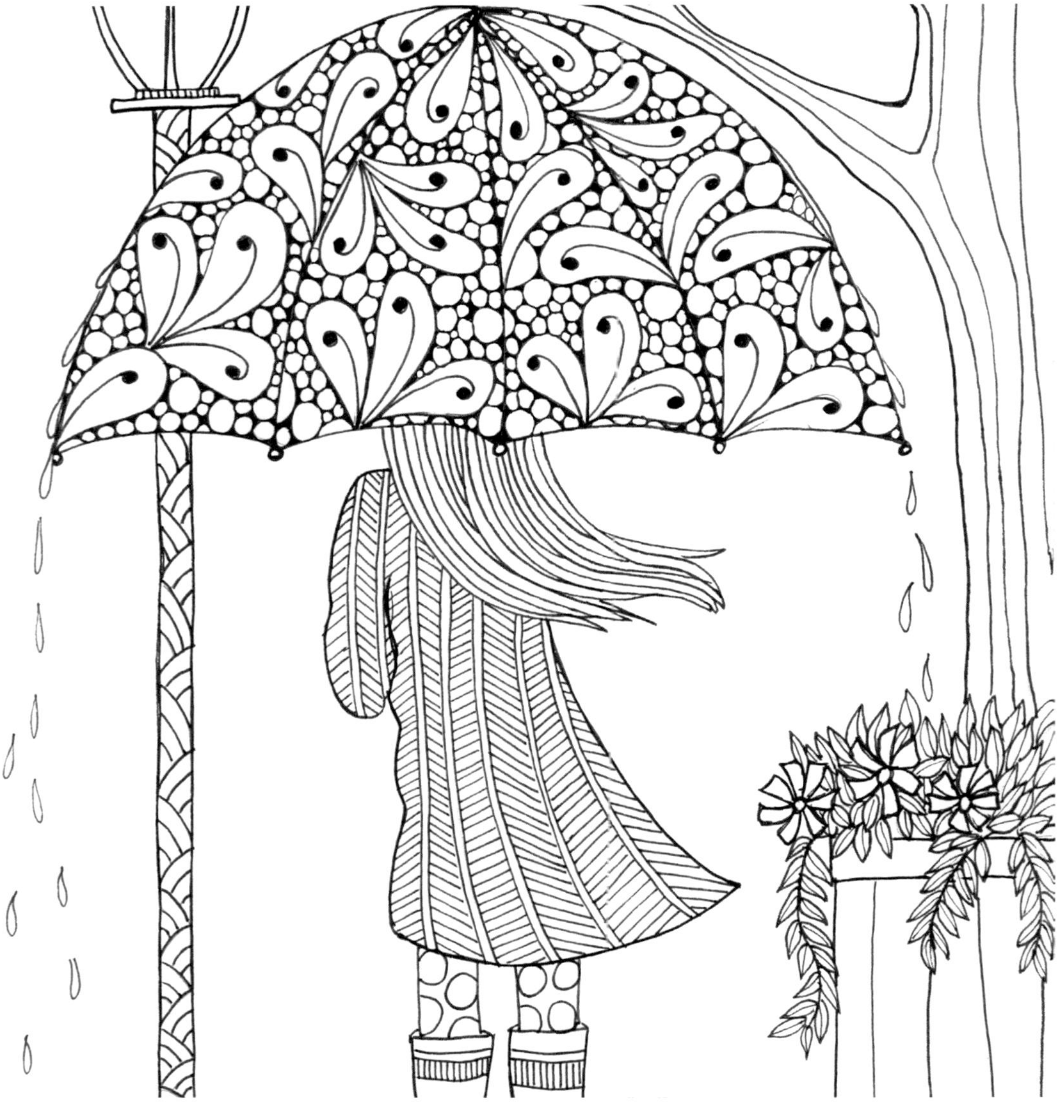

> Be the best version of you
> —Anonymous

there is no limit on versions, keep growing and smiling. how many versions do you think you are on now?

Hard times don't create heroes. It is during the hard times when the 'hero' within us is revealed.

~ Bob Riley

can you sing? write some lyrics to your favorite song here and change them a little bit!

do you sing in the shower like we do?

Each version of you is just as unique as the one before.

Check out this fish... seems she is part bird and what else?

The future belongs
To those
who believe
in the beauty of their
dreams.

— Eleanor Roosevelt

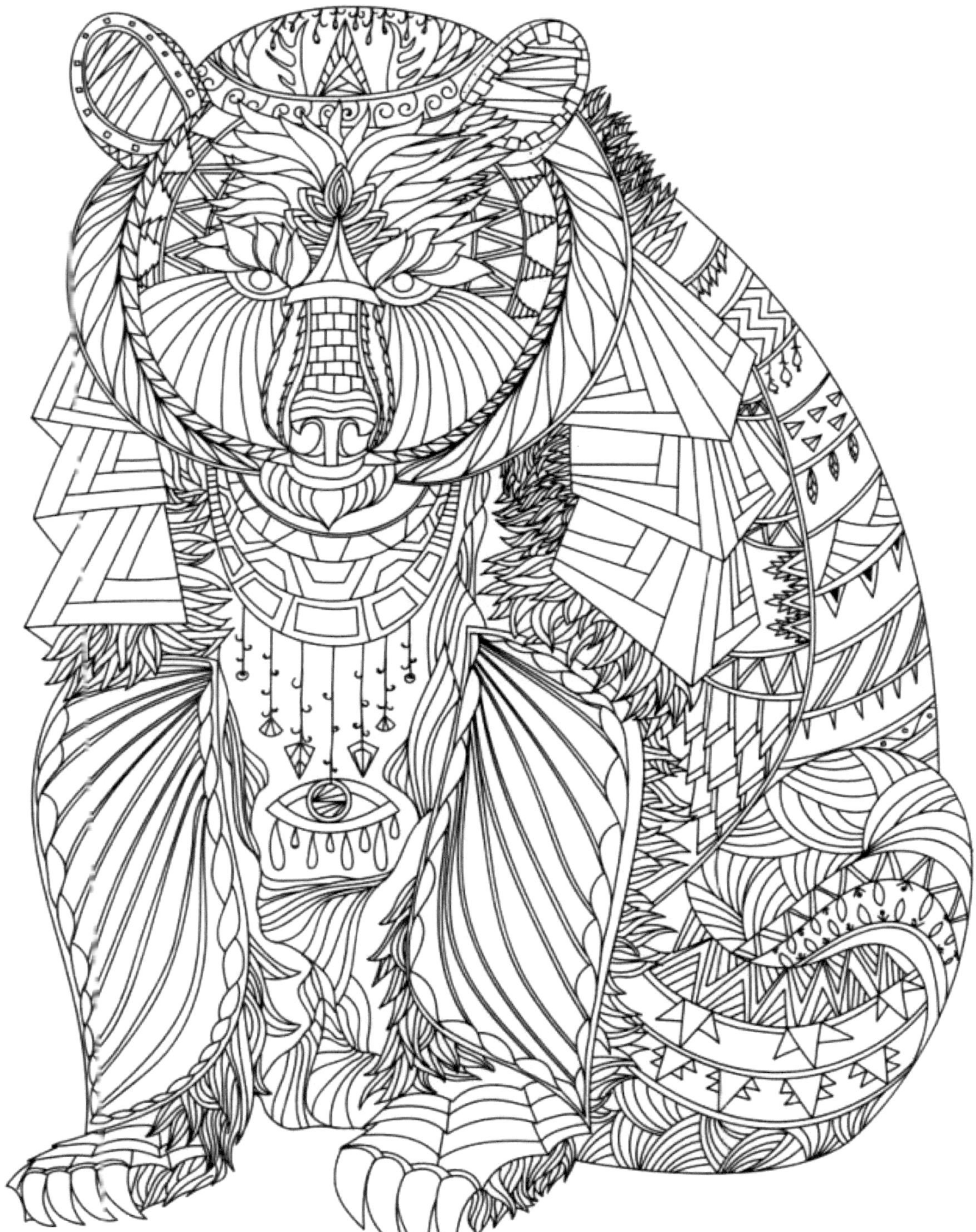

> *let us make our FUTURE NOW, and our dreams tomorrow's REALITY.*
> — Malala Yousafzai

Malala is unique and very driven to make education possible for girls in her country. She is making her future now.

What will you do to make your dreams real tomorrow?

We all take different paths in life, but no matter where we go – we take a little of each other everywhere.

~ Tim McGraw

write the name of someone that makes you feel brave. they go with you on every part of your journey.

why do pencils have erasers and pens do not? you have the power over mistakes, change them, erase them, or start over!

Mistakes are just happy little accidents.

– Bob Ross

"The purpose of our lives is to be HAPPY."

— Dalai Lama

write about what makes you happy...

who makes you happy?

who do you make happy?

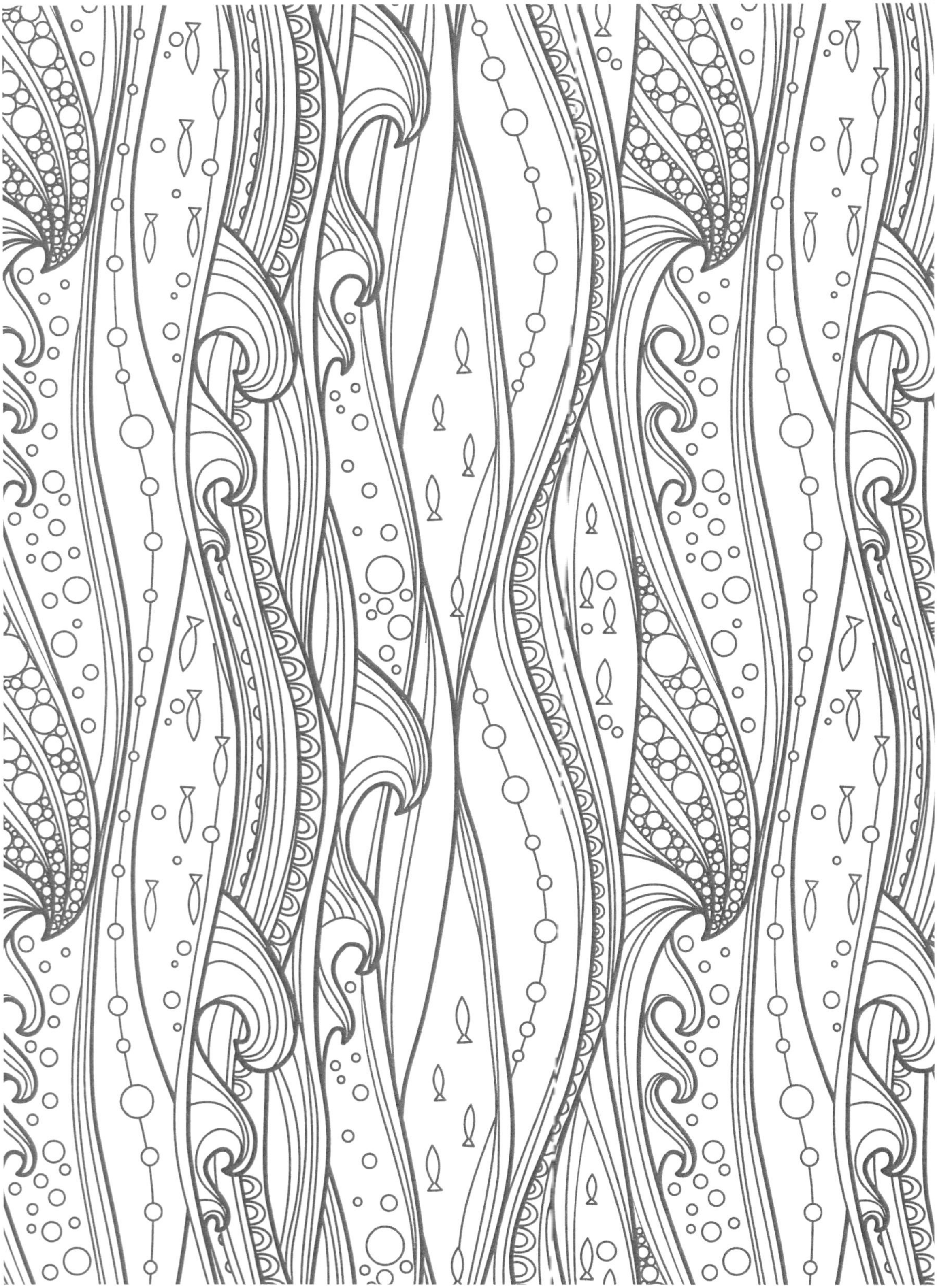

"A CHAMPION is not defined by their WINS, but by how they RECOVER when they FALL." —Serena Williams

Write about the last time you fell and hurt yourself.

Who helped you get up? did you feel better once you got up?

what inspires you? write or draw about it here... oh, and while you're at it, draw some flames to the quote below. thanks!

Be fearless in the pursuit of what sets your soul on fire.

did you feel a bit dizzy coloring this mandala? or does it make you feel calm?

did you ever use sandpaper on a smooth rock? did it change the rock?

write down how it changed...

If you are irritated by every rub, how then will you be polished?

~ Rumi

Your **DREAM** does not have an *expiration date.*

Everything's not awesome, but that doesn't mean that it's hopeless and bleak.
-Wyldstyle

Look outside, do you see a bird? draw & color that bird...

give her a name and a story... is she like you?

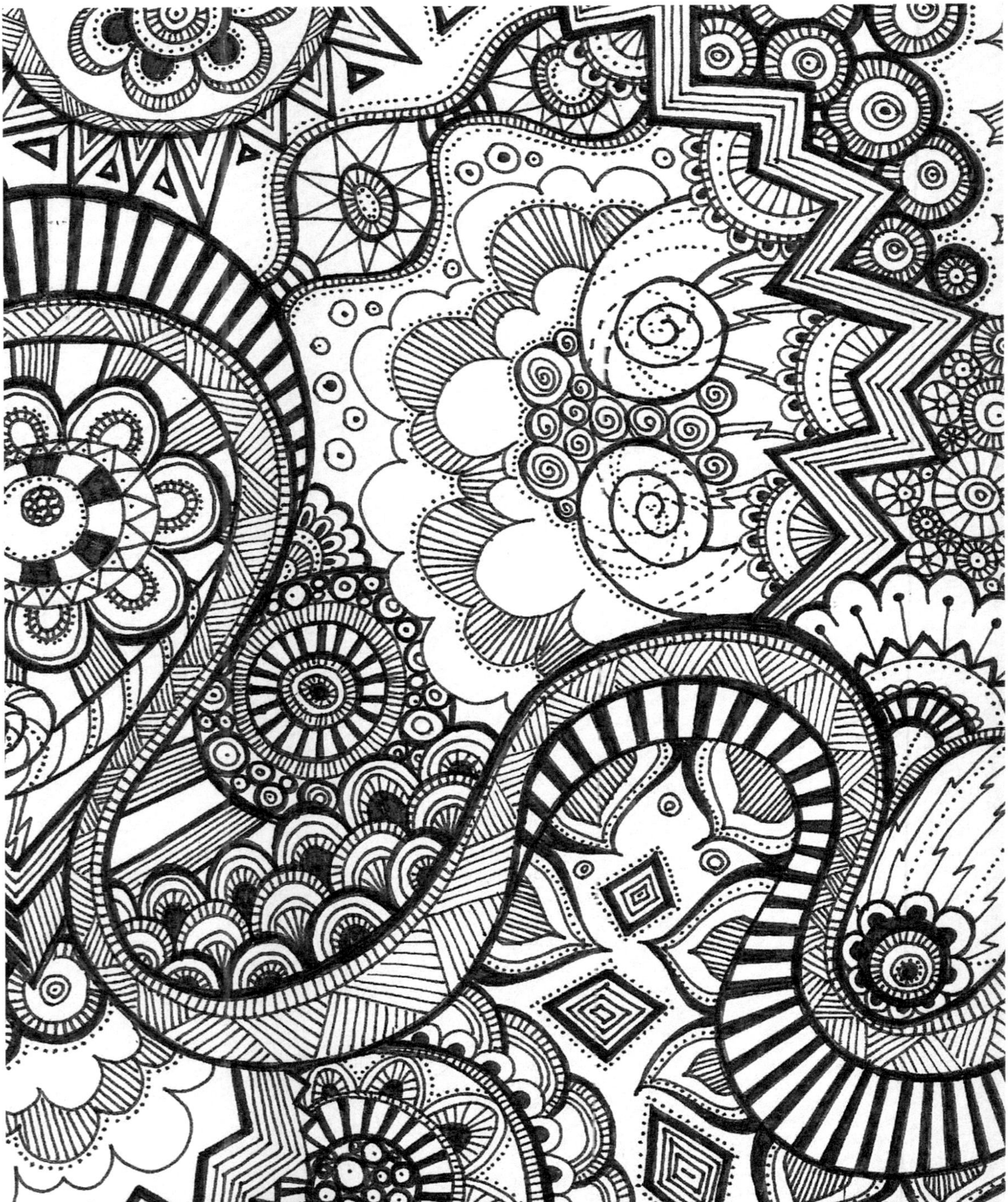

Success is not final, failure is not fatal; it is the courage to continue that counts.

~ Winston Churchill

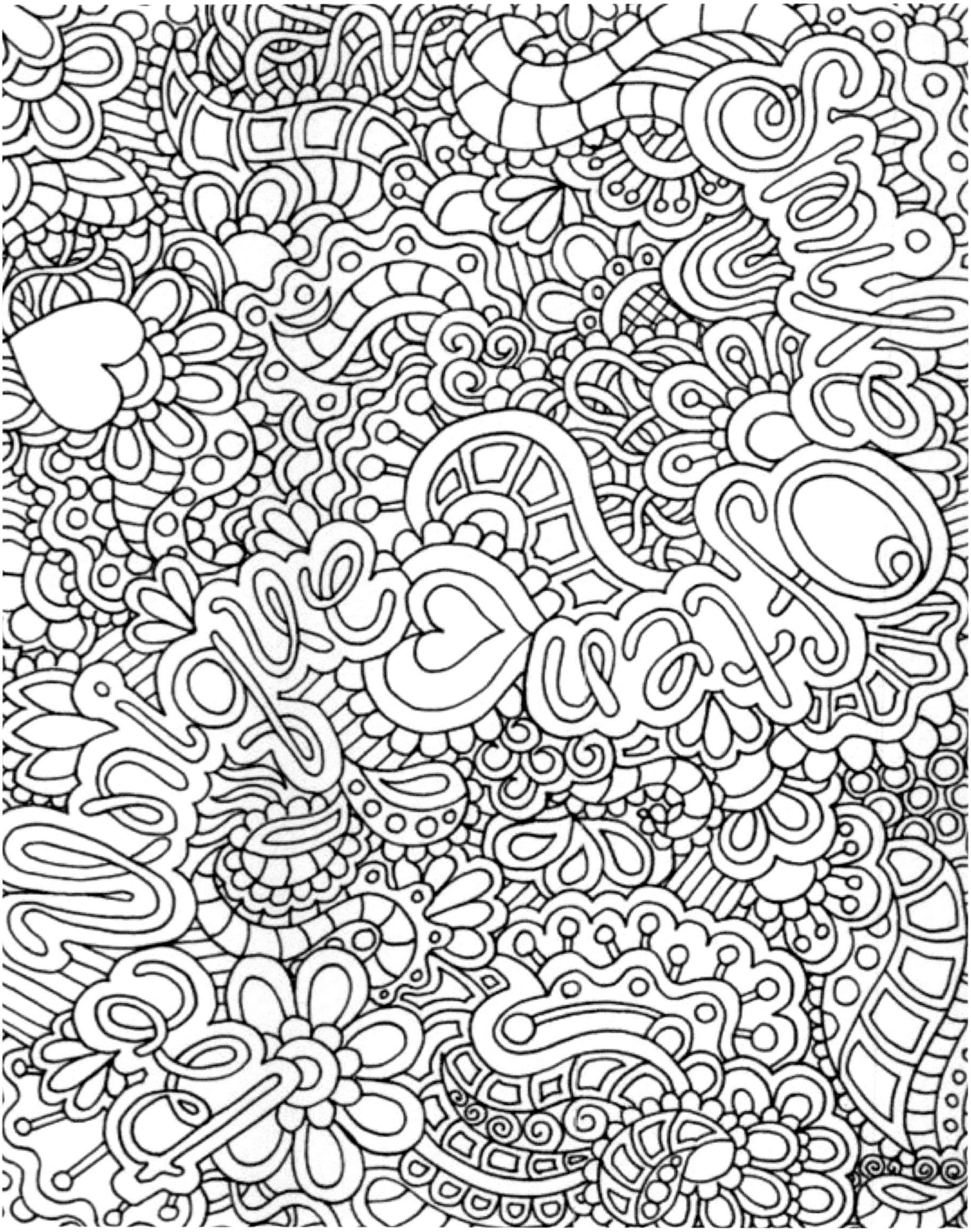

YOU ARE DIFFERENT, SO BE PROUD!

are you proud of how unique you are?
draw something that makes you unique...

To be nobody-but-yourself—in a world which is doing its best, night and day, To make you like everybody else— means to fight the hardest battle which any human being can fight and UNEVER stop fighting.

~ E.E. Cummings

Like the caterpillar that becomes a beautiful butterfly, we all change and become amazing. Smile because you can change too.

Every Time The sun rises, a new HOPE begins

~ Jack

what will you begin tomorrow?

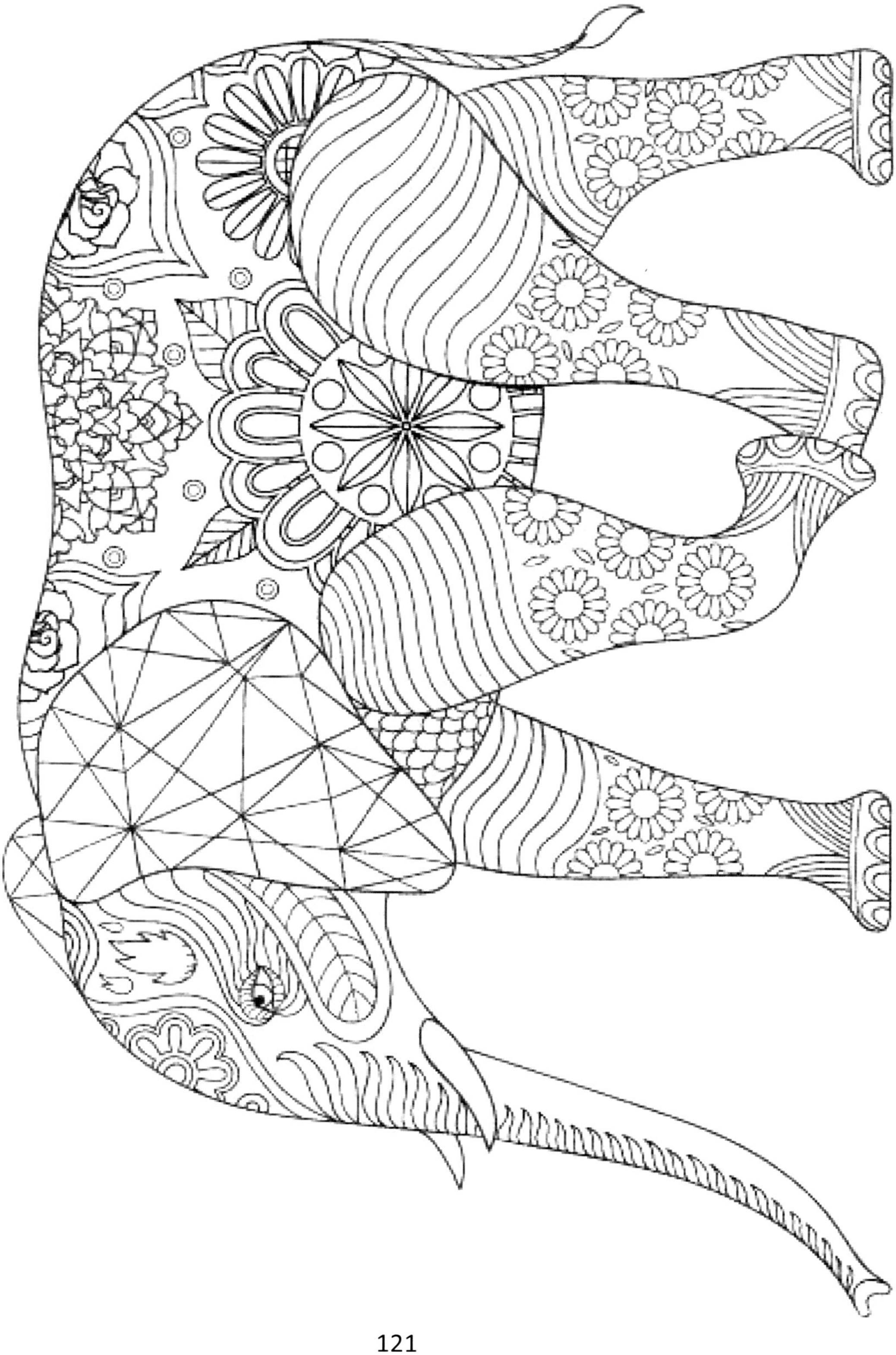

The best and most beautiful things in the world cannot be seen or even touched. They must be felt with the heart.

~ Helen Keller

write about how your heart feels right now... what makes your heart happiest?

Be the one to stand out in a crowd.
Be the one to go where they'd rather not.

Beautiful things don't beg for a chance to glow.
They throw out their lights and just shine out loud.

— Chinonye J. Chidolue

it has been said that comparison is the thief of joy. Choose joy always.

what can you choose right now that makes you happy? colorful markers? a friend? a book?

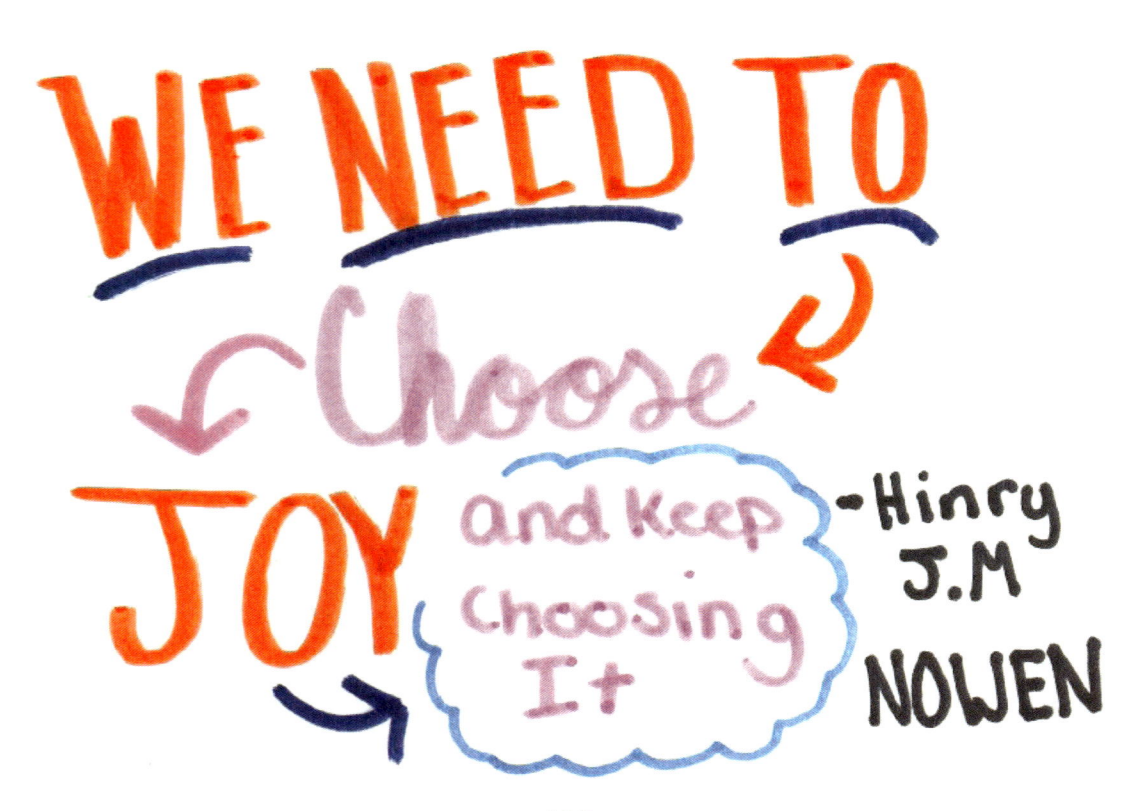

WE NEED TO Choose JOY and keep choosing it

—Hinry J.M Nowen

you are enough
just as you are.

—Meghan Markle

create your own rainbow sentance.
make your own rainbow, your colors –
your way!

Do not go where the path may lead, go instead where there is no path and leave a Trail.

~ Ralph Waldo Emerson

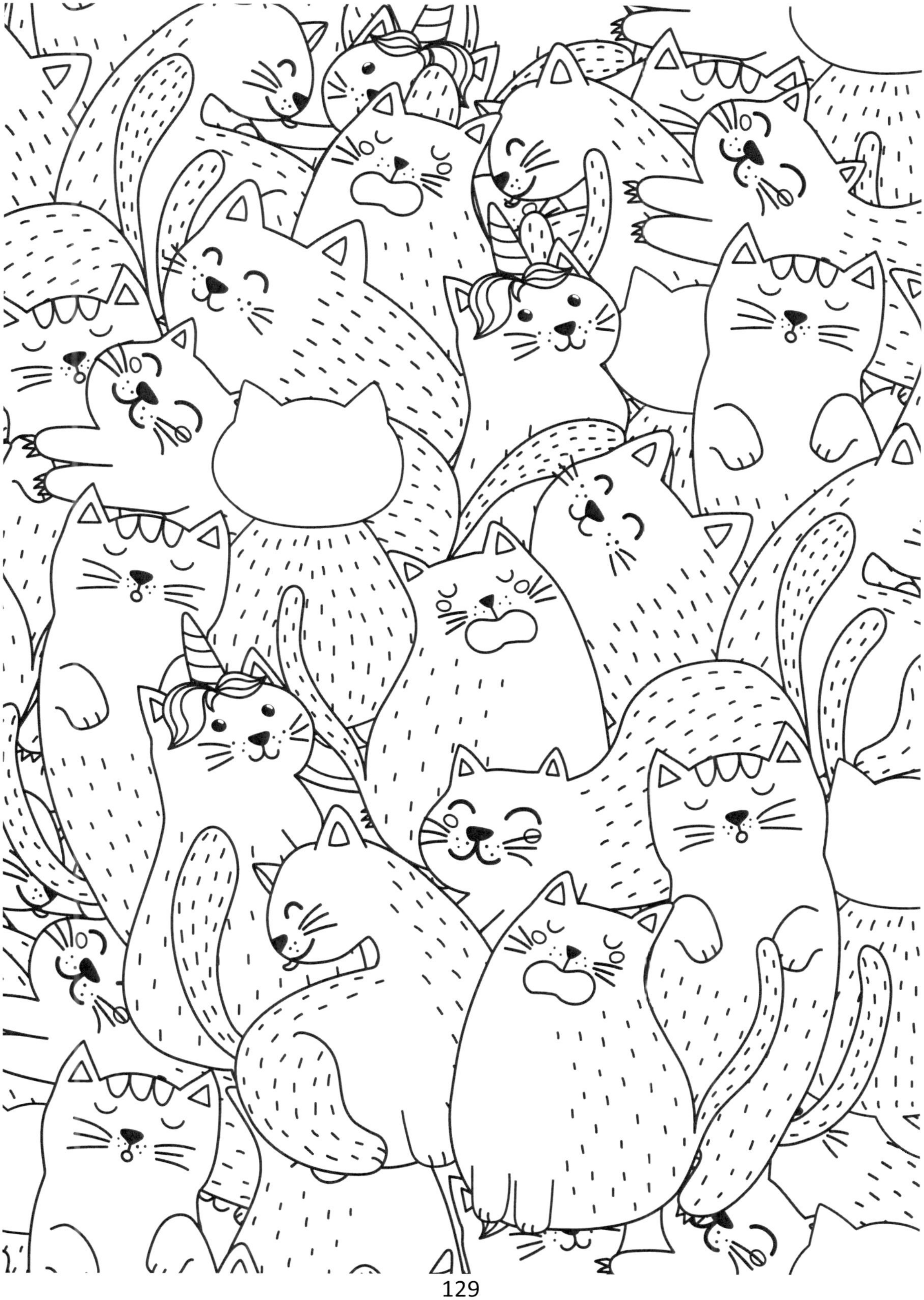

"All our DREAMS CAN come true, if we have the courage to pursue them." -Walt Disney

how would you choose the colors of a rainbow? would it be different? color your own rainbow

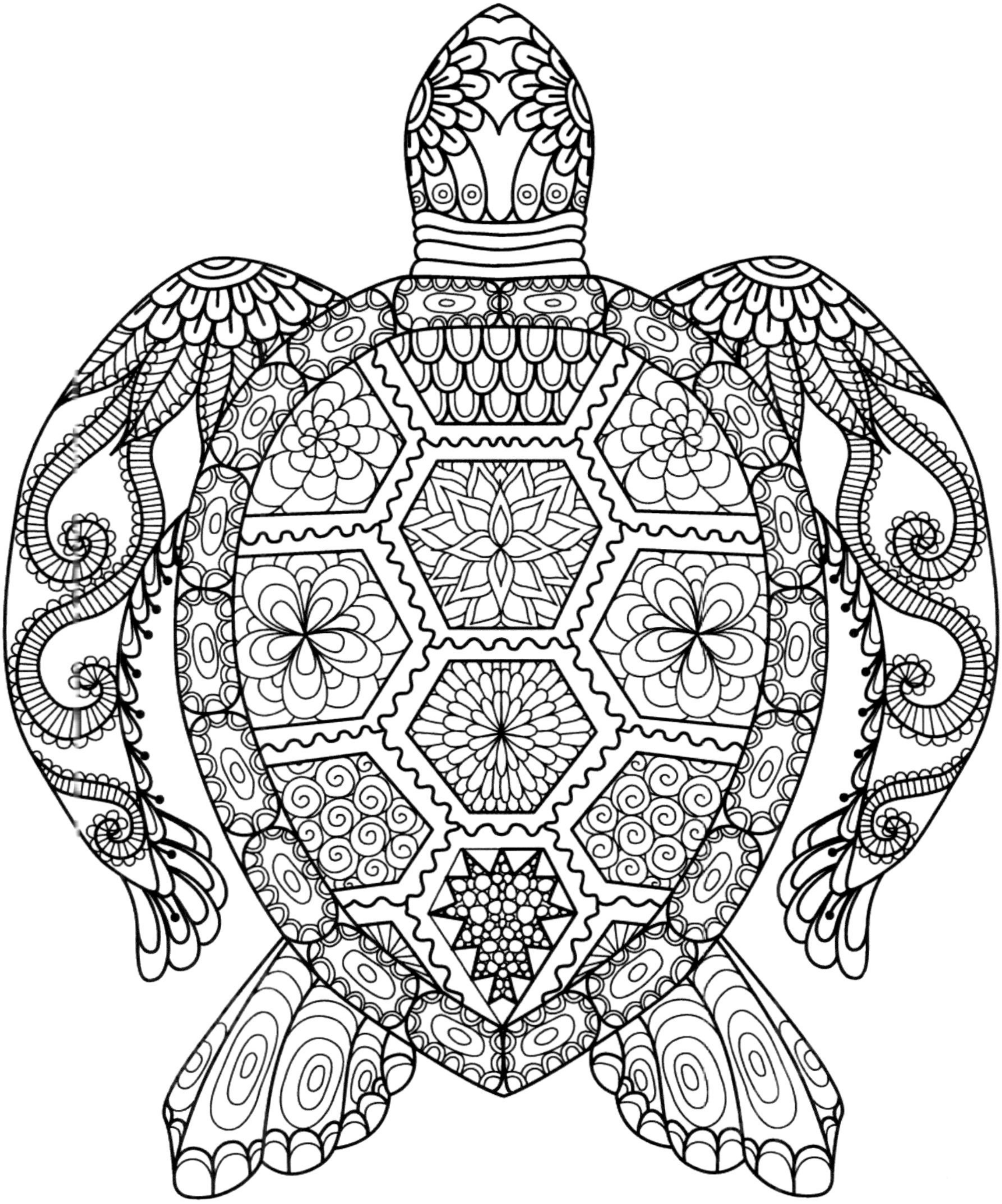

> If I can not do great things I can do small things in a great way
> — Martin Luther King Jr.

Steady and slow wins the race, life is not a competition. Start where you are, do small & great things along the way.

if you could go anywhere, where would you go? write about why you would go there and how.

Can you fly?

The Authors

Page numbers for their favorite quotes shared in this book

Annabelle Nguyen
16, 25, 31, 40, 51, 64, 73, 80, 95, 113

Gracie Vollero
17, 19, 20, 22, 32, 42, 45, 46, 53, 62, 68, 76, 126, 132

Harper Evans
35, 44, 49, 65, 92, 103, 108, 111, 118, 122, 124

Ireland Rodgers
28, 57, 58, 60, 83, 89, 100, 105

Julia Harris
47, 82, 85, 96, 104, 115, 128, 130

Marin McAbee
21, 27, 38

Sara Harris
91

Vivian Harris
43, 70, 79, 117

Zariah Murphy
33, 35, 36, 71, 77, 120

Zoe Rylander
34, 67, 75, 86, 93, 102, 107, 127

The Ladies of Girl Scout Troop #1980

Thank you to Mrs. Penny E. Warren for inspiring us all to be the best versions of ourselves and to keep smiling!

"A bend in the road is not the end of the road… Unless you fail to make the turn."

Helen Keller

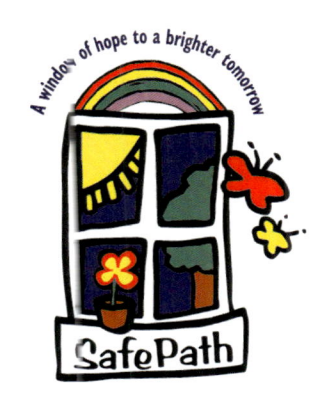

About SafePath

SafePath Children's Advocacy Center, Inc. is a private 501(c)3 non-profit organization dedicated to improving the lives of children who have been abused. SafePath's mission is to reduce the trauma to children and their families by offering a comprehensive, professional, and child-friendly approach to the allegations of child abuse. SafePath ensures a less traumatic, child-focused approach to child abuse cases by bringing together professionals from law enforcement, the district attorney's office, therapists, healthcare professions, DFACS, and other agencies, to all work together as a collaborative team.

SafePath provides unique services for children in our community. While other entities provide food, shelter, and other physical assistance to families in need, SafePath focuses on lessening the trauma experienced by innocent victims of abuse, both children and their non-offending caregivers. SafePath understands and strives to prevent the initial trauma from being compounded by the system designed to investigate, prosecute, and prevent future abuse.

The purpose of the Children's Advocacy Centers of Georgia (CACGA) is to promote, assist, and support the development, growth, and continuation of Children's Advocacy Centers in the state of Georgia. CACGA's vision is that every child in Georgia will have access to the services provided by a Children's Advocacy Center when abuse is reported.

SafePath is a Full Member of the Children's Advocacy Centers of Georgia.